FREEDOM
from the
BONDAGE
of
KARMA

SWAMI RAMA

HIMALAYAN
INSTITUTE®

HONESDALE, PENNSYLVANIA USA

Himalayan Institute
952 Bethany Turnpike
Honesdale, PA 18431

HimalayanInstitute.org

Printed in the United States of America

23 22 21 20 19 18   5 6 7 8 9

ISBN-13: 978-0-89389-031-5 (paper)

This paper meets the requirements of ANSI/NISO Z39-48-1992
(Permanence of Paper).

Contents

Introduction

Swami Rama's lectures on Freedom from the Bondage of Karma were delivered in a seminar sponsored by the Center for Higher Consciousness in Minneapolis. In this edition of those lectures a conscious attempt has been made to preserve as closely as possible the spontaneity and directness with which they were presented originally. It is a mark of the true teacher that as much of profound spiritual truth is conveyed through subtle and personal influence as through words. The lessons are presented here in written form to stimulate deeper reflective analysis by all serious students who seek to understand the meaning of the circumstances and actions of their lives.

In the eight lectures included in this volume, Swami Rama offers a series of perspectives on man's most significant responsibility—that of self-understanding. Karma, the activity of doing and being, is symbolized as a rope of many strands, holding the self in the bondage of suffering and necessitating many reincarnations. The strands of the rope of karma are actions, thoughts, desires and the latent tendencies of personality which lie hidden in the depths of the subconscious mind. The effect of these constituent aspects of karma is to keep the mind in a state of constant agitation and outward-directedness in search of appeasement. The result is enslavement to the many objects, ideas, fantasies and pleasures which vie for the mind's attention.

As long as the mind remains in this scattered and dissipated condition there can be no hope of freedom from karma. But in the pages of this book, Swamiji analyzes the mechanisms of karma and the functioning of mind in order to demonstrate the kind of self-study each student must undertake to free himself from bondage.

In this process of self-liberation three stages are shown to be essential. First, it is clearly shown that the desire for the results or "fruits" of our actions is the root of our slavery. Thus, we must learn to cultivate the practice of non-attachment and of giving the fruits of our actions to the welfare of others. Good or bad actions alike are enslaving; we must learn to live selflessly.

The second essential state of self-enlightenment is shown to be the purification of the conscious and subconscious mind of those desires, thoughts and tendencies which are like a dark veil that keeps us from perceiving the Real. Mind is shadowed by illusion, and freedom is not possible as long as we mistake the non-real for the Real, the non-eternal for the eternal. Yogic techniques are introduced which enable the aspirant to begin the task of self-purification and discrimination.

Finally, it is shown that freedom from karma is to be attained only when one passes beyond the limitations of mind to the highest state of superconsciousness known as tranquility or *samadhi.* From this state alone, achieved through the practice of meditation, the seeker of Truth receives the intuitive awareness of the Supreme Self and passes into freedom. It is the freedom of performing action selflessly, the freedom of genuine love.

Karma is of our own making. What we experience today is the result of what we have created in our past. So, too, is our future of our own making. It is to assist us in the creation of a future that will bring liberation to all who aspire to freedom and Truth that this book is written.

Special thanks is given to Professor Roger Jones, Department of Physics, University of Minnesota, and to his wife for the taping, transcribing and first draft of these lectures. Thanks also to Janet Zima for the cover design and to Theresa O'Brien for typesetting the manuscript.

1

The Rope of Karma

Written on the walls of the great temple of Delphi in ancient Athens were the words, "Know thyself." This theme has pervaded all of human thought. In the West it is the legacy of Greek philosophy, derived from the still more ancient traditions of Eastern wisdom. Everyone wants to know himself and to understand the meaning and purpose of life. It has been the goal of the Indian sages to teach humanity that the problem of life is to know how to live, not only within oneself but in the external world. To live in the world we have to understand the Law of Karma (action) and how to perform our duties.

The Sanskrit word for "action" is *karma*, derived from the root *kri* which means "to do." A man does his action and gets remunerated for it, in turn transferring this remuneration to others for work done by them. Thus, fruit has arisen out of action and action out of fruit. From time immemorial, life has been conducted in this manner. This is called the wheel of karma. To act with the motive of gaining fruits is to invite bondage. Relinquishing them frees us from all miseries. Let us consider how this happens.

If all men understood the value of dedicating everything that they had to the welfare of all beings, no one would be living only for himself. All beings would be linked by their mutual consideration for each other. Those who live for the welfare of all are maintained by the Self of all, the Lord of the Universe.

One who feels delight in giving up the fruits of his actions is a real yogi. Without giving up this fruit, perfection cannot be achieved.

Selfish desire for the fruits of action is the root cause of all miseries. Whoever depends upon the fruits of action for self-satisfaction finds himself bound. In the modern world everyone retains the fruits of his labor for himself. Such grasping possessiveness gives rise to a self-created world of evil and suffering. Only a fortunate few are devoted to the well-being of others and carry out their duties selflessly. The majority of human beings are deeply plunged in grief because of their inability to grasp the illusory quality of the "enjoyment" which they believe will lead to everlasting happiness. It is exactly like a mirage. To extricate such ignorant people from the bondage of misery is indeed difficult, if not impossible.

Before a man understands anything about his actions and duties he must be taught to have a proper attitude. Attitude plays an important role in man's life. Everyone with a secular bent of mind thinks and speaks in terms of "me" and "mine." This is "my house," this is "my property," this is "my wealth," and so on. No one except the person and those close to him are entitled to enjoy this wealth. This is the attitude of modern man. Most of the rules and regulations which govern human society today are designed to preserve the fruits of action. All the governments of the world give protection to the selfish quality in people. Will there ever be a day when man learns to do his action skillfully, giving up the fruits of his action for others?

Very few, however, after understanding the point of view being presented here, will be prepared to forego their so-called rights to the fruits of their action. Alas, speculation about establishing heaven here and now remains a dream for many. If humanity really wants to uplift itself, it will be possible only when it realizes the importance of selfless action and freedom from the strong rope of karma. Humanity needs reorientation; its attitude must be changed. The scriptures declare that there are two paths—the path of action and the path of renunciation. I say the path of right attitude will also help man in establishing a better society.

Karma-phala tyaga is the only principle that can help humanity as a whole to establish everlasting peace. This remarkable principle is to remember to carry out one's own duty no matter what, and without desire for the results. There are three obstacles in the path of doing one's karma successfully. They are:

1. Enjoying the fruits of one's own actions; not giving them away to others.
2. Not doing one's own duty skillfully and selflessly.
3. Doing what is improper, that is, doing what becomes an obstacle in the path of progress.

Due to these obstacles a man fails to progress. Properly understanding and applying three principles will help man in attaining wisdom and liberation from the bondage of miseries-.

1. Giving up the fruits of one's action.
2. Performing one's own duty with skill and for its own sake.
3. Renouncing the desire for self-enjoyment. No one can ever attain freedom without abandoning selfish longings for the objects of enjoyments. It is necessary that one should learn to abandon longings for selfish enjoyments and start doing karma selflessly for the sake of others.

In the path of unfoldment and growth man should learn to expand himself. Such expansion is possible through the enjoyment which is found in selfless action for the welfare of others. One who wishes to secure mastery over his action should learn to do his action so that: first, it does not become an obstacle in the path of enlightenment; second, it becomes a means and a matter of enlightenment; and third, the technique of proper enjoyment becomes an art of living.

Strength is central to this art. However, strength should not be based on the false values presently guiding the conduct of life but on the true nature of the Self within. When man becomes aware of the source of this strength within himself, he will be able to master the technique of enjoying the things around him, yet remain above and unattached to them. The highest pleasure is to find delight in serving others through actions and speech which are known as karma. A man who has learned that it is important for him to know the art of doing his action, naturally wonders what is the precise significance of this action or karma.

Patanjali, the codifier of yoga science, says that having control over the senses, studying the prescribed literature, and turning one's attention to the highest Lord within are the actions to be performed to secure mastery in life. One should practice these disciplines with a view of gaining tranquility and lessening the afflictions of body and mind. There are five afflictions: (1) nescience, (2) self- conceit, (3) attachment, (4) hatred, (5) false pride. Some of the afflictions remain dormant and it takes sincere effort for one to have freedom from their bonds. All the mental attitudes cause difficulty in mastering this discipline, but constant practice helps one in attaining the goal.

Karma is far greater than the mere sum of a person's actions, for it includes both the effects of those actions which are the causes, and the impressions or tendencies created in the subconscious mind by those actions. We speak of the cause and effect relationship between actions and their results as the Law of Karma. This law governs on the plane of human life and consciousness with the same exactness as do the laws of mechanics on the physical plane. Key factors in the working of karmic law are the *samskaras* or "impressions" deposited in the lake of the subconscious mind as a person's character, circumstances and activities. It is the goal of yoga science to liberate men from the bond of karma and to help them attain unity with the Infinite.

Karma may be thought of as a rope of many cords, twisted together to give it strength. The rope of karma is inextricably woven into the fabric of every life-, it binds all who breathe. The harder we struggle to escape from the rope of karma, the stronger its grip becomes. To become free from it, we must gain knowledge—knowledge of the Self, of the mind, and of the Truth within.

Most knowledge is obtained from the external world through sense perceptions, training by parents and schools, from neighbors and the traditions of society, and so on. All such knowledge is called in Sanskrit, *apara vidya,* knowledge of this shore. *Vidya* means "knowledge," *para* means "beyond," and *a* is a prefix of negation. Thus, *apara vidya* means knowledge not from beyond but from here. Only *para vidya* or knowledge of the beyond will lead to enlightenment and liberation. *Apara vidya* is the kind of knowledge normally obtained through the process of reasoning and from the contact of the mind and senses with the material world. For *para vidya* the serious aspirant needs to unlearn all that has been learned in this way. In order to gain the knowledge which will free him from the rope of karma, he must first become free from all he has learned and has been in his life so far.

In this unlearning process, it is found that unconscious knowledge is much stronger than conscious knowledge. If a person is told not to meditate on a monkey, it is predictable that he will spend most of his time in meditation preoccupied with the monkey. This illustrates the unconscious component of all learning. The conscious mind is very crowded, and merely training the conscious mind proves of very little value in obtaining higher knowledge. We must get through the superficial levels of the conscious mind to the unconscious mind. The important question is to what extent this is possible. Can we consciously train the unconscious mind? This question is a frustration to many who would be teachers, especially yoga teachers, for it implies that the true knowledge of a yogi is largely unconscious learning and cannot be transmitted verbally or intellectually. Much of what passes for knowledge is mere imitation which does not help us at all in gaining higher knowledge and freedom from the rope of karma. A true yogi will teach his students more by example and subtle influences than by verbal communication.

Most of what we receive as knowledge from the external world has a disturbing effect on the mind, much like the disturbing effect of a pebble breaking through the mirror-like surface of a still pond. Thus, the first step in significant learning is not a great leap by which wisdom is instantly attained, but rather the act of becoming free from disturbances on the surface of the mind. The seeker must do this for himself; no one can give him ultimate wisdom or the state of enlightenment called *samadhi*. He must light his own lamp. To do this, it is first necessary to become free from what one has created both consciously and unconsciously. For the most part these creations are actual barriers around the Self. Consequently, most of such learning does not lead to enlightenment but rather serves as an obstacle to such an attainment.

It is the karma created by a person's own actions, not by any cause external to himself which is responsible for his present condition of life. It is of no avail to blame God, fate or circumstances. The fact that an individual suffers from past acts is not a disparity in God's law but the failure to order his life by the law within his own being.

Nor does much praying or wishing help. Going around all day saying, "God, God, God" does not help to change a person's condition any more than a child can get what he wants by crying, "Daddy, Daddy, Daddy" all day long. Conviction is more important than belief- conviction that through seeking we may help ourselves. Belief is no consolation in a time of crisis. One's own beliefs often prove to be fragile and disappointing. Belief in God which is mechanical, and appeals to Him for "favors" cannot yield freedom and liberation. The aspirant must continuously prepare himself for receiving true knowledge, knowledge that will enlighten and liberate him. He must look for the deeper levels of knowledge beneath and behind the superficiality of fact and cognitive experience. This is illustrated by the three levels of teaching in the Bible. The first is what might be called ordinary teaching. It can be understood by most people regardless of their state of preparedness and is exemplified by much of what is contained in the Old and New Testaments as history, laws, and factual data.

The second kind of teaching is for disciples, that is, for those who have undertaken a disciplined program of preparation for enlightenment. An example of this is the Sermon on the Mount or Christ's statement, "You must be perfect like your Father." Most people are unprepared to hear these words, for they are unwilling to strive to overcome their imperfections. Buddha and Krishna, as well as Christ, tell us that we may be free from imperfections but belief in gods and religious faith are not enough to help overcome the imperfections in ourselves. Rather, we must become students of life. We are helpless unless we study our own actions, and to do this properly it is essential to follow the second kind of teaching in which the meanings and implications of actions become clear. Such teaching is found in Christ's great sermons, Patanjali's codification of yoga psychology, and the Bhagavad Gita.

The third kind of teaching in the Bible is the highest, and it is called *revelation.* The Book of Revelation is in this category. This book seems to be based on the experiences of John. The Book of Revelation tells us that Christ revealed his great Truth to His beloved John. Revelation is knowledge which can be received only by one who has achieved a high state of purity and preparedness. This knowledge comes not through intellectual ability nor through the conscious mind, but by an act of grace, achieved through one-pointed mind, self-purification and meditation. Revelations are possible only for one who has known and experienced truth directly. Such a person is a *guru.*

In the Book of Revelation we read that the Book of Life is sealed. Who is it that opens the seals? It is not a man, nor a god, but a lamb. This teaches the importance of humility and the need to purify the ego. The lamb symbolizes the elimination of imperfections and the attainment of perfection. It also suggests the process of preparation that is necessary to perceive the Truth. Normally society teaches people to inflate and worship their egos. To receive revelation or truth it is necessary to reverse that trend by purification of ego-centered consciousness.

The Book of Revelation also teaches that direct experience is the true source of knowledge. A great master teaches only on the basis of his own experiences. True knowledge does not come from without, but only from within. A disciple may complain and say, "My teacher is not showing me God." But the teacher will answer and say, "First tell me what kind of God you want to see, and then I will show Him to you." The choice belongs to each individual; each must decide what it is he wants to know. Each seeker must perfect himself. Do not expect the guru to do these things for you. The disciple must view himself as though standing on the bank of a river, asking, "Who am I?" as the river of life flows before him.

Too often people brood over the past or fear the future instead of learning to live here and now. We should not dwell on what is irretrievably past or on what may never come. We must strive to eliminate the space between our thoughts. Once this space has been eliminated, time is also eliminated, and without time there is no causality. Life should be like a stream; it should flow without a break. The water that has gone by and that which has yet to come should be of no concern. Only the present should occupy us, filling our every moment until we expand into the consciousness of the whole stream which remains stable and ever-present despite the flux of what appears to be change.

In studying the philosophy of life, we discover that man is in the bondage of karma. Whenever you perform an act, the fruits of which you desire or seek to acquire, you become bound by that act. All actions are binding as long as we are not free of their fruits. Even the fruit of good deeds binds us. You cannot attain freedom by doing good while you are still attached to the results of your good deeds. Incidentally, in the Eastern view, "badness" or evil is not seen as a separate force as it is in the West. Evil is imperfection, but not something that exists in and of itself. We should not regard ourselves as lost sinners. Feeling guilty only gets in the way of our growth towards perfection. Our task is to become free from attachment to the fruits of both good and bad deeds. The state of freedom from bondage is the state of perfection.

Yoga teaches us how to perform actions without becoming attached to their fruits. We seek the fruits of our actions only because we are unaware of our real needs. There is just one need which really matters—to attain freedom from the state of misery. That is what Christ meant when He said, "You must be perfect like your Father." This doctrine is also central in Hinduism and Buddhism. To begin the journey toward freedom we must analyze the nature and source of the cord of action and of the other fibers which lie beneath it. Anything that happens in the external world is preceded by something happening internally. Conscious or unconscious thinking precedes all acts. Therefore, we need to examine the nature of thought in order to thoroughly understand our actions.

How can we free ourselves from the heavy cord of action and the finer cord of thoughts? To see the relation between these two cords, we should note how easily the mind wanders and is distracted from our actions. It is common for us to do one thing while thinking of something else. Our actions do not determine our thoughts. Rather, they are governed by the thinking process either at the conscious or the unconscious levels.

The thinking process, in turn, is regulated by the even finer and stronger cord of desire which lies beneath it. Below that lies the subtlest and strongest cord of all, the cord of impressions, or in Sanskrit, *samskaras*. There are the primitive emotions, urges, and tendencies that motivate our entire lives. They are the impressions carried from our past lives in our subconscious minds; they motivate our desires, and there in turn produce our thoughts and ultimately our actions. These cords are all intertwined in the rope of karma. It is from the bondage of this rope that we seek liberation.

Thus, liberation means freedom from our own ignorance. To accomplish this our self-study must unfold on all levels—actions, thoughts, desires, and impressions. These may be partially analyzed with the help of the rational faculty or scripture, but we remain limited on this plane by our limited experiences. We cannot transcend the field of our confined minds. It is only through a self-study based on performing our actions skillfully and selflessly, on meditation, and ultimately on the discovery of the immortal Self within that we can achieve new levels of experience and knowledge. These are the methods of yoga.

This kind of self-examination can help us. Self-unfoldment is the only pursuit by which we may free ourselves from all miseries. Our incarnation in a body on the physical plane provides the opportunity to undergo this self-examination and attain liberation.

The physical brain acts as a source of energy. The nervous system channels this energy so that the body can function. A good mind needs a healthy body and nervous system in order to operate and govern the process of life and self-development. The purification methods of yoga help us to achieve this necessary state of health. Purification of the nervous system allows us to penetrate deeper than is normally possible into the pool of the mind. As we proceed, we find that disturbances rise up from the bottom of the pool. Confrontation with our impressions, desires, and thoughts becomes unavoidable as they surface in our awareness from the deepest levels of the pool of mind. It is to these deep levels of the mind that we must plunge in order to root out all sources of disturbance and see our true nature. There we will also find Truth and achieve liberation.

2

Mind—The Finer but Stronger Cord

Before anything happens in the gross world it is preceded by something happening in the subtle world. Actions move first within the mind because the mind is subtler than the body and thoughts are subtler than actions. However, the link between action and thought is not a straight-forward one. In both the Bible and the teachings of the Buddha there is awareness of the subtle cord of thinking which lies beneath the cord of action in the rope of karma. Buddha said, "Whatever a man thinks on, that he becomes," and Christ meant the same thing when He taught His disciples, "Where your treasure is, there shall your heart be also." We tend to become what we think, and our thoughts normally reflect the karma stored up from the past in the vast storehouse of the subconscious. Therefore, to free ourselves from the bondage of our thinking, we must become aware of how our minds work. The mind itself is like a busy workshop which keeps us from being aware of our soul and spirit. Thus, it is necessary to understand and regulate this mental workshop so that we may realize soul and spirit.

Right learning begins with the awareness of ignorance. He who claims to know all is a fool. A wise, humble person admits that he knows nothing. Such a person really does know something. Gandhi said that most of the important things he learned in his life were learned from children. Children have spontaneous cognition based more on instinct than on intellect. Thus they are closer to intuitive knowledge and to their true nature than adults. We must strive for this quality of the child's mind. We begin by concentrating on that which keeps us from knowing the Truth, namely, the mind itself. We will find that God is already known. It is ourselves whom we must come to know and understand in order to realize our true nature.

By studying outwardly the nature of karma, we cannot understand its inner essence. We should remember that the whole of our body is in our mind, but the whole of our mind is not in our body. It is the mind that makes hell and heaven for man. Mind is a means of enlightenment if it is understood with all its functions. To attain perfection means to have perfect mastery over the mind and its modifications. It is necessary for everyone to elevate himself. In this respect there is very little aid coming from without. We all are eager to bring about our own elevation by attaining spiritual heights. No one wishes his own downfall, but few and far between are those who sincerely follow the path. Ordinary persons imagine that others would help them rise. Most often we say that Mr. "A" helped me immensely, but Mr. "B" brought about my ruin. This, however, is not the right line of thinking. Can it be said that millions of people who are crying today have themselves created all their miseries? The correct answer to this question is "yes." Each person is himself the creator of his own happiness and misery.

Man is a citizen of two worlds—the world of his own thinking and the world surrounding him. He reflects his inner ideas on the world outside and perceives things as he wants, not as they are. For example, if you study relationships in the external world by studying wife and husband relationships, you will come to know that they blame each other for their own deeds. They reflect their thinking on each other and make themselves unhappy. If all the relationships are properly understood the flower of life will bloom in delight.

In India, marriages are arranged for enlightenment rather than for biological necessities or physical love. This does not imply a coldness or lack of understanding on the part of Indians but rather the greater emphasis placed on people's uniting for spiritual attainment and companionship. Ram Das said, "Oh mind, follow the path of devotion." Much more human energy must be directed towards this great purpose. This can be done through the art of inner conversation and observation. Uncontrolled thoughts lead to the asylum, but controlled internal dialogue leads to an understanding of the nature of the mind and helps in the path of meditation and contemplation.

What, in fact, is the mind? What are its different functions? In modern education emphasis is placed on one specific aspect of the mind, namely, rationality. We take great pride in this function and use its creations to enhance egocentric consciousness, the great enemy of genuine spiritual insight. We must study and develop aspects of the mind other than the rational in order to become aware of our ignorance and prepare ourselves for true knowledge.

There are various ways of studying the mind. According to yoga psychology, mind is understood by understanding *vrittis,* which are modifications of mind. Patanjali, the codifier of yoga science, sets a definite program of training the mind and its modifications and thus leads a student to a state of *samadhi.* He gives four definite steps of training the mind: *pratyahara* or sense withdrawal, *dharana* or concentration, *dhyana* or meditation, and *samadhi* or self-realization. These are gradual training steps for transforming the entire personality.

In Patanjali's system training is emphasized more than analysis. According to yoga psychology, the exclusive analysis of external behavior (as pursued by some schools of modern psychology) is an inadequate method for fruitful understanding of the nature of the mind and brain. What is required is to delve into the thinking process to find out how to deal with the problems which arise in connection with our thoughts and actions. The main approach of modern psychology and psychiatry is to help man by working on his emotions, whereas yoga psychology trains man on all levels—the physical, mental and spiritual. By studying behavior or the emotions we really do not probe into deeper levels of our mind. Simply expressing emotions is not sufficient training to attain emotional maturity. It is important to stress the fact that no modern psychological concepts show the way of transcending the subconscious mind. If the time comes when these branches of psychological science talk of transcending mind, they will have to accept the established methods of meditation which have been systematized in yoga science for millennia.

In meditation many things come into our awareness and disturb us. For example, we may find ourselves caught in a collision between the personal and collective mind in which we are disturbed and troubled by others as we try to meditate. Through the continued practice of meditation, control over our mental agitations is achieved. To meditate is to be fully alert. The mind becomes one-pointed. Mental activity and thought become continuous like the pouring of oil from one vessel to another. We may be aware of and concentrate on each drop of oil, yet there is also continuity. There is no break in our thoughts. Through meditation the personality expands towards union with all things. It expands towards the universal *I*. We learn to see the same reality in all things—in a snake and in a swami alike.

The other states of our mind lead us astray, and we must constantly strive to overcome them. Dreams, for example, function to fulfill our desires. When our inspirations and desires cannot be translated into reality, we dream about them. So dreaming is simply an expression of our suppressed wishes. Dreams are based on the truth but they do not tell the truth. For a swami, on the other hand, there is no difference between waking and sleeping; he has no suppressed desires and therefore no need to dream. Sleep and dreaming cannot change our personalities, but *samadhi* can.

The superconscious state can make a sage even of a fool. Because the gurus have attained the superconscious state, their teachings and wisdom are to be treasured. They are like transmitters of eternal knowledge and light. They receive and transmit this higher energy to us. Reverence for the guru is thus not reverence for him personally, but rather for the light and knowledge communicated through his material body. It is not enough, therefore, to worship the guru in his material form or through rituals. We must treat his suggestions and teachings as true light and knowledge being passed on through him from the long line of gurus extending back to the source of ultimate Truth. This Truth may be obtained only in the fourth state, by gaining complete one-pointed control over the mind.

In dealing with our thinking process we have to face many problems of the train of thoughts which have various forms, symbols, images, ideas and fancies and which actually have their root on the deeper levels of our minds. We can term them all passions. Our passions are the root cause of our emotions, and we need to be sincerely working with our passions. For example, a story is told of a swami who was directed by his master to visit another teacher so that he might learn to overcome his angry temper. After a long search the swami found the new teacher on a remote mountain. He appeared to be dead. The swami spent much time probing and testing to see whether the teacher was dead or alive and finally, after convincing himself that the teacher was dead, he left exasperated. As he descended the mountain, he heard a voice calling him back, and he returned to find that the teacher was indeed alive. The swami threw himself at the teacher's feet, asking to be forgiven for how he had treated him while testing whether or not he was alive and begging for help in overcoming his problem of anger. The teacher promptly kicked him right in the chest and knocked him half-way down the mountain side. The swami got up angrily and ran back to the teacher, filled with rage and violence. As the swami raised his fist the teacher said to him, "You can leave now. Obviously, you have no control over your anger. What good are all of your supplications and entreaties? You became angry just because I kicked you down the mountain. Is that how a man of inner peace, a swami, behaves?" This story shows that in the method of yoga psychology the teacher not only teaches us to look into ourselves and find our problems, but he gives us practical lessons and helps us develop strength to overcome these problems.

What happens to us when we become angry? We are enveloped with a cloud of ego and selfishness. It is like a fire of passion, an abnormal mind-engulfing state. We must unlearn these habits, and to do that we not only analyze ourselves but also follow reliable methods and techniques to help us overcome these problems.

Study of the *Mandukya Upanisbad* helps us to understand the mind. How do we know what we know— that we have a mind, that others exist, and so on? All such knowledge comes to us during the course of the waking state. In this state the senses are coordinated with the conscious part of the mind. If the conscious part of the mind is not coordinated with the senses, then you are either dreaming or in a state of meditation. This normal waking state is the one that is emphasized in the process of education as it is normally practiced in the West, with great value placed on rationality. According to yoga science, as mentioned earlier, there are four states of consciousness: the waking state, the dreaming state, the sleeping state, and *turiya,* the fourth state.

Turiya or *samadhi* is the state of true knowledge and realization. In the absence of this state we remain bound by the rope of karma. In fact, some animals function more effectively in nature than man. For example, animals can instinctively sense such dangers as earthquakes. Their minds do not intervene to inhibit the natural operation of such instincts. They are often better able to cope with problems and difficulties than humans. The human mind on the other hand is so crowded that it cannot be guided by nature as animal minds so easily are. Furthermore, in the West so much attention has been placed on the waking state that knowledge of how to use the dreaming and sleeping states for learning is virtually non-existent. In some of the families in India even today children are educated in their sleep. If the parents know the method of sleep learning, they can help the child to grow when he is asleep and then sow the seeds of *samskaras* (impressions) in his mind. A child's mind is like a tender bamboo for it can bend easily; while adults' minds remain preoccupied.

Modern Western thought tends to view the non-rational aspects of mind as irrational; the suprarational is feared and avoided as if it were infrarational. It is this tendency which has kept the West of today entirely ignorant of the powerful educational capacities of the fourth and highest state of intuition.

Only a small part of our mind is studied and utilized in the waking state, leaving the totality of mind unexplained and unutilized. Life can be deepened by intensifying inner meditative experience and, in a parallel manner, by grounding our outer actions in the great subtleties which flow out of such experience. We are all limited by the sum total of the experiences accumulated up to a given point in time. The mind cannot go beyond whatever it has seen, heard, imagined or studied. However, through meditation it is possible to gain new and extraordinarily valuable inner experiences which help further our growth. It is necessary, however, to discriminate carefully between the variety of experiences called *inner* so that this growth can be authentic and meaningful. Visions and hallucinations, for example, do not transform our personalities, however much they may excite and impress us. People who believe themselves to be possessed by devils are, in fact, suffering from a lack of confidence and from hallucinations. Learning to use our whole mind serves to protect us from these fascinating but wrong kinds of experiences. This is what is meant by the biblical injunction, "He who has ears to hear, let him hear." We must develop the ear and eye of the whole being. At present we see only with our physical eye, not with the real eye of our mind and soul.

To correct this the superconscious state of *samadhi* must be reached; the waking state is not enough. The sages all knew that *samadhi* was necessary because they had lived in and experienced enough different states to know the advantages of each. Through their own experiences they had learned that true knowledge comes only in the fourth state, the state of superconsciousness. The world will not improve in any significant way without learning new uses of the mind. Only through achieving the fourth state can man become divine. It is necessary to expand the mind to this state in order to attain realization and peace.

Consider the mind as existing on four levels. The first and second levels are the ones on which we operate in everyday life, namely, the conscious and unconscious levels. These are the levels on which thinking is done and where the senses and the conscious mind operate in coordination with each other. The third level is the subconscious level. We are normally unaware of the activity going on at this level where all of our memories and past forgotten experiences, emotional urges, desires and impressions are stored. The fourth level, that for which we are striving, is the superconscious level—the state of total awareness.

The conscious mind is easily trained. It is affected by external stimuli and occupies our attention most of the time, but it is more difficult to train the subconscious mind. In order to reach the highest level, the superconscious state, it is necessary to gain control over the subconscious level. To do this the conscious mind must first be calmed through meditation so that the subconscious contents can begin to surface. Thus meditation has a threefold purpose: first, to calm the conscious mind; second, to teach us how not to be disturbed by the flood of images arising from the subconscious mind; and third, to go beyond the conscious and subconscious mind to the highest state of *samadhi.*

3

The Thinking Process

As we have seen, the mental cord in the rope of karma is stronger and finer than the action cord. It is easier to control action than thought. It is essential, however, that we learn to control the thinking process; otherwise freedom cannot be attained. By gaining control over the thinking process we can gain control over the impressions stored in the mind and eventually over our entire karma.

Through introspection (inspection within) one can discover the nature and origin of his thought. Mental functioning and internal motivations always precede external actions. We often do things mechanically out of habit, i.e., as a result of ingrained mental patterns. Through introspection we can learn to understand and see clearly our habits and their origins. The word *personality* has its roots in the Latin word *persona* which means mask. This refers to the masks used by players in ancient theaters to *personify* certain character types for the audience. We make our own personality. It is a mask etched by our character which is itself determined by our habits. Through introspection we can change our habits and thus change our character and personality. In order to change habits we must be aware of our present condition and our goals. The goal is simply to be perfect. As we grow through introspection our conscience makes us more aware of our perfections and imperfections, and we gain greater control over our mind. If our acts and thoughts remain unchanged, then we display a distracted personality; we experience a lack of coordination between mind and body, between thinking and action.

To bring about the changes necessary to affect one's habit, one must attain the state of *turiya* or *samadhi,* which is resisted out of fear of the unknown part of the Self. It helps to recall that this unknown mind is of one's own making, that you are not your thinking process, you are the thinker. Without changing your habits, you cannot change your personality or your thinking process. Through introspection, through observation of what effect your habits, thoughts and actions have upon you, you can learn to distinguish between what is advisable and beneficial and what is harmful or dangerous for you. You can learn what is your real nature and what is not your real nature.

In our essence we are pure, wise, free. It is because of our identification with the non-eternal that we become imperfect, like a pure person who is corrupted by evil friends. We can approach the process of discrimination by introspection into the procession of symbols, ideas, images and fantasies in the mind. We see right away that the participants in this mental procession are not independent of one's life. For example, symbols are forms or representations of things within the imagination. These symbols have certain inner meanings for us. We color them ourselves, and we cannot trust them without correctly analyzing them. So there is right knowledge and wrong knowledge. Yoga science never asks us to follow anything blindly but rather to discriminate and to analyze. Learning to discriminate between useful and harmful knowledge is an important facet in the process of introspection.

That which is supported by facts is right knowledge. That which is not supported by facts is wrong knowledge. Thus sense perceptions form the first rung in the ladder of knowledge. Even the senses, however, must be supported by facts. When under the influence of an hallucination or a fantasy, we may believe that our senses are telling us things which others cannot corroborate; therefore we must be discriminating. We must be sure that the facts support the knowledge gained through our senses. Much of what comes to us in meditation is wrong knowledge. It simply occupies our mind, forces us to dwell on things that are disturbing us and prevents us from finding the calm and peace which we seek.

Very often people complain when they see nothing during meditation. They should, in fact, be grateful for this. If we see things in meditation, then how does meditation differ from life? In everyday life we are constantly bombarded by sense perceptions. Meditation teaches us how to get away from this, how to find peace. What good would meditation be if we were to continue to see things and to have our minds occupied by the same thoughts which we have in our normal waking state? Normally we see a great deal when we try to meditate—the fantasies and symbols of our mental procession. We can eliminate these things by learning not to be affected by what we see.

Meditation is not thinking and worrying while sitting. Rather it is learning to cross the boundaries of the personal and collective mind. Here we must follow Patanjali's Yoga Sutras and become introspectors, observers and witnesses of our own thinking process. We must learn to become fully conscious and to be in control through meditation. Meditation is consciously bringing forward knowledge from the unknown part of ourselves, from the infinite library of knowledge within us. Meditation does not make you passive; it makes you dynamic and creative and allows you to unfold your total personality within and without.

When a meditator learns not to identify himself with his thinking process and his train of thoughts, he becomes aware of his essential nature and starts witnessing things differently without any identification. The meditator is not disturbed by the actions and attitudes of others. This state requires that we learn the different functions of the mind. According to yoga psychology, the mind has four major functions. The first is *manas,* which is the importer and exporter of the perceptions received from the senses. It is the doubter. It is what we normally refer to when we speak of the mind. The second function is *buddhi,* which is the intellect, the discriminator. The third function is *ahankara.* This is our false sense of ego, that self which we incorrectly identify with our thoughts, actions, and thinking processes. And the fourth function is *citta,* normally called the subconscious mind. It is the place where all unconscious memories and emotions are stored.

Manas is like the foreman in a place of business. It employs many functionaries but dislikes taking orders from the other parts of the mind, particularly from *buddhi,* which in principle should be the discriminating and decision-making center. *Manas* should be asking, "Shall I import or export? What is good for me or bad for me?" *Manas* must learn to listen to the *buddhi.* We must sharpen our *buddhi* and learn how to make decisions. We must use our intellect to overcome our habits.

The next set of problems is usually associated with the ego or *ahankara.* The ego thinks that it is the owner of the business. This is the part of the mind which requires purification, transformation into the Supreme Soul or the Supreme *I,* Purification means surrender of the ego and placing it at the disposal of the inner Self. Remember that conquering the ego does not mean suppressing or destroying it, but rather enlarging and expanding it. You must ask in any given thought process or action, "Does my ego get in my way or not?" You must learn to use this question to distinguish useful from harmful thoughts and then to surrender the ego when it is causing a problem. The ego has forgotten its association with the Supreme Self. The ego has created its own bondage, a great imprisoning fortress, which can be conquered through surrender to Self, to God, to the reality within. We must learn to deny the ego when it insists on having its way or on dominating the Self and the mind. Growth requires penetration to the deeper level of intuitive knowledge. We must learn to gain control over all functions of mind, making it integrated and one-pointed.

Finally, the *citta* is the unconscious storehouse. It is like a vast screen on which we paint our impressions or a huge lake into which we drop pebbles or impressions derived through the senses from the external world. To see what is stored in the *citta* and to learn how to deal with and overcome it, we must first calm the conscious mind. This is why we must constantly observe the thinking process and see what its nature is. We generally find that the thinking process is supported by wishes, wants and desires which are not all the same. Wishes generally involve doubt. We are not certain we can have that for which we wish. Wants are usually unreasonable. They are demands for things which we either do not deserve or are impossible for us to obtain. Desire stems from need. It usually expresses the necessity to fulfill some urge or craving. All of these things must be examined and sifted through. We must decide which is good for us and which is bad, all the while observing the train as it passes by.

Without the total integration of all our faculties we cannot cross the boundaries of the mind and soar to higher levels of enlightenment. One of the functions, either the ego or the *citta,* will dominate and keep us from reaching our goal. When we meditate we must always think, "I am thine and thou art mine." This must be spoken to the inner Self. This must represent the surrender of the ego and all that we have. We can accomplish this by repeating our mantra, by inspecting our thoughts and by learning to transcend all artificial beliefs.

It is necessary to learn how to follow the true teaching of the Bible, "You must be perfect like your Father." We must learn that we are the children of eternity whose purpose is to grow toward that realization. From reading the Bible, the Gita and other great scriptures we can learn the inner meaning of life, but we have to understand what is really meant. For example, Christ left the Jews not to condemn Judaism but rather to bring about a revolution, to give man real understanding. That understanding is Christ-consciousness or Universal consciousness. This can be learned from the Bible or from yoga or from the Buddha. Christ, Patanjali and Buddha all had the same aim. They teach us that we are striving for inner knowledge of the Infinite Self.

No great man has ever attained self-realization or God-consciousness without the total integration of mind. If mind is not made one-pointed and inwards one cannot peep into the deeper levels of the subconscious mind and go beyond the mire of delusion. Unless the mind is an integrated one it cannot perform skillful actions, because the finer cords of the thinking process and desires will remain obstacles in the path of liberation.

To attain freedom from desires a right method of meditation is very important, and for meditation we must learn to purify our minds. We do this through self-observation, introspection, witnessing and practicing the science of word or mantra. The science of word is found not only in yoga teachings and scriptures but also in the Bible and in Buddhism. The first initiation, or act of grace, is a mantra initiation. It is through word and sound that we are led ever inward to the deeper meaning of the Self. Word has sound; sound creates ripples; ripples produce form and form has meaning. That meaning responds when we need a friend or guide, and it can also lead us deeper and deeper toward the inner Self. The science of mantra is one of the definite methods which is introduced by the teachers and gurus. It is through mantra that we shall be led to the inner experience of the highest state of awareness.

4

The Law of Karma

We cannot live without creating thoughts and performing actions, yet these very thoughts and actions entangle us in the net of cause and effect. However, freedom from karma, which means to be free from the bonds of cause and effect, is possible despite the inevitability of our actions. To cross the ocean of *maya* and ignorance and reach the far shore of wisdom, we must learn to perform our actions skillfully and selflessly. To help us achieve this freedom it is of great assistance to study the law of karma and how it affects our lives.

Karma is the expression of the rule of perfect justice within us. It is the law of the cosmos reflected in the microcosm, man. There is nothing arbitrary or punitive about it; it is universally the guarantee that every act produces results which finally return again to the source. Karmic results may be immediate or delayed, but they are always inevitable. Such is the truth behind the verse in the Bible and in the Gita, "As you sow, so shall you reap."

It is a mistake to think of ourselves as individuals who live only once as mere products of favorable or unfavorable circumstances which seem to surround our present existence. Actually the Self is reincarnated into many lives due to the necessities of karma. Reincarnation is a strange concept to many in the West because it seems alien to Western culture and traditions. Reincarnation is not discussed in the Bible as it is in many of the great scriptures of the East. However, even in biblical times reincarnation was taken for granted by many throughout the East and Middle East. Christ refrained from openly teaching the concept of reincarnation to His uninitiated followers so that they would not develop fatalistic attitudes. Reincarnation has been known and mentioned by others in the West from the times of ancient Greece onward, and many philosophers such as Plato, Hegel and Schopenhauer accepted this concept. For Plato, reincarnation was an important metaphysical principle since, according to his teachings, knowledge is built up in this life on the foundation of learning and experience gained in previous lives.

The concept of karma leads to the conclusion that nothing happens by accident. This is not a fatalistic idea, however, since whatever happens is both the result of previous choices and actions and is necessary for completing the experience of the individual. What happens to us is the fulfillment of what we have done in the past; what is to be in the future will likewise be the result of present actions. The karma created by previous action cannot be altered. We can, however, determine future karma.

The advantage of reincarnation in human form is that it provides the one reborn with a certain degree of free will which can be used for spiritual progress and for overcoming the bonds of past karma. To see how this free will operates for human beings within the laws of nature, it is necessary to understand that there are four kingdoms in the cosmos: the human, the animal, the vegetable, and the kingdom of clay and stone. Human life affords the opportunity of evolution towards a certain destiny, that destiny being determined by ourselves alone. When we become dependent upon the fruits of our actions, our destiny takes a form which may necessitate many additional lives; but through selfless actions liberation can be achieved in this life. Animals, in contrast to human beings, have instincts that guide them in their actions so that their lives are largely governed by the laws of nature and not by themselves. Vegetables are even more inert; they have fewer instincts, but they are alive. (Vegetables are quite sensitive, however. They can even communicate and experience emotions.) Natural law is more dominant in the plant kingdom in the sense that plants have less control over their destiny than animals.

The extreme case of non-control is that of the kingdom of clay and stone. Non-living matter is completely subject to natural law with no trace of self-determination. Average human beings, in contrast to the other kingdoms, are in a state in which perhaps fifty per cent of their lives may be controlled by themselves. Enlightened people have complete control over their lives. We are as we are because we want it to be that way. In effect, we have earned our present condition; and each incarnation gives us new opportunities to create more favorable circumstances for future spiritual un-foldment.

Rebirth in a human form is the necessary condition for gaining experience by which the consciousness of the Self may expand into full awareness of its essential unity with God. Through the operation of the universal law of karma, the Self is born into those conditions which enable it to gain the necessary experience and to complete the work left undone in previous lives.

The law of karma and how it affects an individual may be represented symbolically as a man firing arrows from a bow. The arrows already released, like past karma, are no longer under control. They are a person's present fate. There was control over them at one time, which determined our fate in the past. Present karma is not out of our control—it is in our hands. The arrow that is just now being loaded in our bow is the one which can be controlled. If this is done skillfully and selflessly, the arrow will reach its mark. We no longer control our childhood, yet we are living out the consequences of that childhood. It follows that to control the present in which we live is also to have some power in the determination of our future. If attachments can be burned up in the fire of knowledge through selflessly and lovingly performing present actions, a desirable future can be created. The law of equality and retribution in nature can always be understood in terms of the law of karma.

If we cannot completely dissociate ourselves from the fruits of our actions, we can at least surrender them to humanity. The skillful gardener who gives the fruits of his labor to his master, overcomes his karma; but the obsequious gardener, who praises his master and gives him nothing, remains in bondage. This is how we should all act; we must relinquish the fruits of our actions and stop worrying about them, for if we spend all of our time worrying, we will have to return in another incarnation and go through the whole process again.

As long as we look only at the effects of karma it remains a mystery. We must look for the root cause, and to do this we must try to understand the nature of free will. This requires that we learn what we mean by the terms *wish, want, will, desire,* and *impressions.* A wish always contains an element of doubt; we are not certain that we may have what we wish for. A want includes an urge, there is a feeling of compulsion behind them. Want is the offspring of craving which has its roots in the subtle impressions called *samskaras* which we carry with us from the past. They are the results of our past actions whose fruits we sought to possess and could not relinquish. It is the attachment to our desires and the results of our actions that give such strength to the rope of karma.

It is said that the face of Truth is hidden by a golden disc. This golden disc is a symbol for all of the temptations of life and for the subtler cord of the rope of karma, the cord of mind or thought. This cord is finer but stronger than the first cord of action for it involves more of the inner world, in particular, emotions and feelings. Emotionally we are like fish in a turbulent lake. Most of our responses are reactions to the environment which surrounds us. When our bodies are pleasantly stimulated we are pleased and call it love. When we are hurt we call it pain or hate. We are constantly affected by these outside influences and respond to them like fish caught in a current. We must learn to live in our inner world and to establish peace and tranquility which is not affected by any outside forces. Living too much in the world of others prevents this from happening. Our education and culture leave us no time to delve into our own inner world, free from outer disturbances.

Food, sleep, fear and sex are the basic determining factors of personal emotions. All of these primitive impulses are controlling and affecting us in different ways. A dream involving sex, for example, may satisfy us while a dream involving food does not. This is because sex has its greatest effect upon the mind, whereas a dream feast cannot nourish the physical body. However in one way or another, all of these external influences disturb our mind. We are more acutely aware of our responses to the external than to the internal world. The external world is allowed to control our lives and retard growth. How? We are afraid of exposing ourselves and thereby revealing our weaknesses to others. Consequently we rarely have the opportunity to correct personal defects. Two-thirds of our personality is beyond our awareness and control. We live with others but do not come to really know and love each other because of our inability to really learn about ourselves. Instead, we love others to satisfy ourselves. We expect others to dance around us as a nucleus. We look to the whole outside world for satisfaction because we have never learned to explore our personal identity and true needs. We think that this whole world belongs to us but never admit that we belong to others as well. We may share the same bed with someone, but we dream differently. Others are rarely allowed into our private world. We want more time to spend in our private world but become frightened upon entry and run back to others. We must learn to explore this world and to share it with others.

If you love someone, that person cannot hurt you; yet we seem unable to share inner experiences with our loved ones. Stronger fences are built around ourselves to keep our loved ones out than the barriers created to control strangers. When people live together it takes longer for them to adjust to each other because their inner lives are more exposed. This period of adjustment is not generally understood, and people often give up and try to find someone else with whom they think they will be more compatible. It is better to try to correct that which is known than to search for something unknown. An unknown devil is worse than a known devil.

How can we become free from the tyranny of emotions and our primitive urges? We must learn to be unaffected by others and try to understand the purposes of our lives and actions. All eat—dogs, men, swamis; but why do we eat? Learning how to eat and why to eat is an art. It is something which must be understood and controlled. Why do we want to live? Indeed, we should all aspire for a long life of one-hundred years or more, but for the sake of enlightenment and not simply for enjoyment or pleasure. Control over ourselves means learning to regulate ourselves physically, mentally, and emotionally. We must learn how to do and how to be.

Relying on external stimuli always leaves the mind scattered and dissipated. A distracted mind is somewhere else; there is no control over it. There is, of course, both a voluntary and an involuntary part of the mind; but the mind is not yours unless you can control it in all respects. A master can control all the processes of his mind, whereas most of us belong to and are under the control of our minds rather than vice versa. In other words, our mind motivates our actions and because we are not free the fruits of these actions are being reaped constantly.

To gain control over ourselves the exercise of will is necessary. This in turn requires a study of the relationship of the body, the mind and the soul. Will power is not a separate source of energy apart from us and our minds. Will power implies a certain state of the mind. Normally our minds remain in a scattered and dissipated state; when the mind becomes concentrated and one-pointed we have will power. A disturbed and dissipated mind has no power to will. He is master of himself who has understood the different functions of the mind and has gained control over all of them.

What is unique about the karma of a great yoga master? Like us, he too has a certain purpose in life, certain actions to perform. Such a master is not completely free to choose the course of his life but understands perfectly what he is doing and why. He is carrying out his duty but is not enslaved by it; there is no reaping the fruits of such action because they are offered to mankind and God. He is like a potter who continues spinning his wheel after completing his pots. He is totally absorbed in doing his actions skillfully and selflessly and freely gives away the results of his actions. The only concern is to make the pots firm and beautiful; not to possess them. Everyone must perform actions in life, but the secret is to learn to do them without reaping their fruits.

In the rope of karma, mind is a finer and stronger cord than actions. In the West, in the science called psychology, we learn much about certain aspects of the mind, emotions, cognition, volition, etc. In the East the mind is dealt with differently, as in Patanjali's Yoga Sutras and in the Vedanta philosophy. Yogis approach the mind through experience. They have learned to study the inner states of mind in terms of their own meditational experiences and have firmly demonstrated the existence of a fourth state of mind, that of sleepless sleep, of equilibrium and tranquility, which is called *samadhi* or Christ-consciousness. In this highest state man can attain total understanding and control over himself. How was it possible, for example, for Christ to change water into wine? He could do this by entering the fourth state in which He attained complete mastery over Himself and the situation. In this highest state Christ could express His love to all people and things, and just as the beloved blushes before her lover, so nature "blushed" before Christ, and water became wine.

Meditating can teach us all of these things. If people come to meditation for narrower or less meaningful reasons than those we are suggesting, then let them begin in that way. Sooner or later meditation will lead to a higher path. The true purpose of meditation is to awaken people to the greater reality within them. Meditation leads us to seek enlightenment by performing our actions skillfully and selflessly. Ultimately the desire for enlightenment swallows up all of the urges and desires of the lower ego. Enlightenment becomes the highest of life's goals.

5

Samskaras

Samskaras are the dormant traces of our past karmas, actions, thoughts, desires and memories. Yogis know that the life breath links the mind with the body. Similarly the *samskaras* link the soul with the subconscious mind. When the life breath ceases, the subconscious mind and the soul separate from the body, the five active organs, the five senses and the conscious portion of the mind. This separation does not mean complete annihilation. Our *samskaras,* having all the potential of past memories, thoughts, and deeds, remain latent in our subconscious mind. It is the subconscious mind which is the vehicle in which the soul travels from this plane of life to another plane. Death is actually a mere separation.

As long as the soul uses the subconscious mind, that storehouse of merits and demerits of our past lives, we cannot become free from our karmas at all. An analogy will clarify this. When the wind blows it carries away the scent from a particular place or object, though the source of that scent is not carried away by the wind. When we leave our body all memories in their subtlest forms are carried away by our subconscious mind, and we go to another plane of existence. These memories and subtle thought forms, which contain the seeds of motivation for our life after death, are responsible for rebirth.

Put another way, in the river of life all our actions, thoughts, and sensations are like pebbles which settle on the bed of the river, and we soon lose conscious awareness of them. These pebbles or sensations thrown into the river create very tiny bubbles in the depths of the river which come up and burst at the surface. All our *samskaras* reside in the latent bed of memory. When we start studying life with the help of contemplation and meditation, these hidden *samskaras* come up to the surface as if seeking to be expressed in the external world. If we become fixated on these bubbles of thoughts which arise in the river of our life we will be unable to achieve liberation. To study action and even thought can provide some personal consolation; but it is not the way of liberation and enlightenment, although it is always helpful to understand one's actions and thoughts. Without focusing on the subtle traces of our mind stuff, that is, on the *samskaras* in their latent form rather than on their manifestation at the surface, salvation is not possible.

When a student, after withdrawing his senses, starts meditating and calming down the conscious mind, he experiences the bubbles of his thoughts rising to the surface; but he is not aware that all these bubbles actually originate in the bed of the river of his mind where disturbing pebbles are constantly settling. He often resists these disturbances and can become disgusted with himself on account of them. If the student is patient and determined he will cease to struggle with these thoughts and will start to study them. This study needs careful attention so that the rising thoughts do not adversely affect the student. This is possible if he practices witnessing the thoughts by not identifying himself with the quality, image, idea, fantasy and fancy which appear before him and which can entice him. It is natural for all the hidden tendencies of our subconscious mind to come to the surface, and it is also natural for a student to be disturbed by them. Yet if the student remains aware of his goal, which of course lies beyond the subconscious mind, then he will learn to study these thought forms without discomfort. Past *samskaras* do create problems and disturbances for the student of meditation, but sincere effort, determination and one-pointedness can help him maintain awareness of his goal. Constant and exclusive study of the thinking process at the conscious level is not a sound way to follow the path of meditation. It is self-study of the subconscious mind or mind stuff which is important. Many strange thoughts rise to the surface during our thinking process and it is not possible for anyone to analyze and get rid of them at the conscious level, for these bubbles form deep in the subconscious mind.

When the aspirant endeavors to cross to the other shore of life and enter the Kingdom of the Soul, these *samskaras* create obstacles for him. Our mind ordinarily operates on the conscious, unconscious and subconscious levels. In meditation the mind is allowed to proceed beyond these levels to what yoga calls the superconscious level. If the strong motivations and subtle traces of our past *samskaras* prevent us from going beyond our personal minds, how can we proceed in a practical way to cross to the other shore of life and achieve realization of our true Self?

To begin with it should be clear that *samskaras* motivate our whole lives in the external and internal worlds as a result of our own deeds, thoughts and choices. No one punishes us for our good or bad deeds, but our past *samskaras* motivate our present actions. The way we sow is the way we reap; this is the law of karma. In fact we punish and reward ourselves. When we understand our *samskaras,* the motivating force within us, then we can not blame others, nature or God for the life that we lead. Man suffers on account of his karmas, thoughts, desires and *samskaras;* and his greatest suffering is bondage to the rounds of birth and death through which he is led by them.

Often people seek to analyze the karma in their relationship with the people with whom they live, but that is only one aspect of understanding karma and the fruits that are received therefrom. Karma is a law of our own making. One cannot live without doing karma, but it is also true that one cannot live without reaping the fruits of one's own karma. One is bound to receive the fruits of his karma, and again the fruits motivate him to do fresh karma. Then how is it possible for one to gain freedom from these karmas?

There are two ways of gaining freedom from the bondage of karma. One is to renounce karma; the other is to do karma skillfully and selflessly. It is not practical or possible for the ordinary man to renounce all of his duties, eliminate his desires and surrender his motivations; but the practical way of gaining freedom is to do one's own karma skillfully and selflessly so that karma no longer remains a bondage.

The path of selfless action done skillfully is the practical path for most people. There are a fortunate few who follow the path of renunciation by treading the path of knowledge and not following the path of action. People in this world are not all the same. One class of persons derive benefit from the path of renunciation, another from the path of action. The path of renunciation is for those who are firmly established in the path of knowledge, but not for others. The path of action is therefore of greater practical value for most of mankind.

Those fortunate few who are extremely detached remain aloof from the desire for enjoyment. Those who have no sense of attachment in the very essence of their nature devote their life to the attainment of knowledge alone. They renounce all their duties solely for the sake of attainment of absolute knowledge. It is only to such rare persons that the path of knowledge is of use in securing their ultimate goal. All deeds and actions are inspired by desire, and desire is motivated by *samskaras.* Any acts done with the view of increasing one's pleasures affect our karma, but deeds done without any desire do not affect the doer. When acts inspired by desires are given up, this is called renunciation, or self-restraint, i.e., to completely give up all the desire-inspired actions that are calculated to increase one's desire for enjoyment. Therefore in the path of renunciation one has to curb, to give up, one's desire for enjoyment. One who treads the path of renunciation does not give up all actions but only those actions which are inspired by the desire for pleasures. In the path of renunciation one cannot give up actions which would benefit the world or contribute to world peace. Desire-inspired action means desire for enjoyment, and this desire for enjoyment is a desire for one's own selfish enjoyment. No one can renounce the desire for eating or for other actions necessary for the maintenance of human life. In the path of renunciation the non-acquisitive attitude helps and results in the increase of happiness. Thus in the path of renunciation giving up all deeds, actions, and karmas is not necessary, but only those actions must be given up that are inspired by desire for pleasure.

Karma, studied on the basis of *samskaras,* also will reveal the nature of the work which one has to do. By performing some duty or action after careful study of the inherent promptings of the *samskaras,* one can slowly cross the river of ignorance of *maya,* following the strong currents which originate in the *samskaras.* It is not possible to fight against the strong currents of *samskaras* or escape from them. It is better to find the way and swim across by following the pattern of *samskaras,* doing one's duty to get to the other shore.

One should never renounce one's duty through delusion, emotion or ignorance. Blind renunciation will never help the aspirant. Giving up one's duty or karma causes misery. A man needs a few essential necessities to live; thus the necessary effort to gain one's livelihood has to be made.

We have already described how actions are motivated by the thinking process; our thinking process, by our desires; and desires, by our *samskaras.* Our thinking process travels along three avenues: *tamas, rajas and sattva.*

When action is endued by *tamas* one becomes inert and starts acting negatively. This state of sloth is very dangerous. Action endued by *rajas* also gives fear of pain, and one remains in a state of insecurity and conflict. This is the main cause of affliction, and most often when one's action is endued by *rajas* one is led toward selfishness, which is one of the main causes of self-bondage. When sattva-endued action is performed without any desire for personal enjoyment and gratification, then that *sattva-vritti* motivates our cognitive senses and the organs of our body to function harmoniously and leads us to a state of tranquility. In this state the doer does his action without any personal desire of pleasure, doing his action for others pleasantly and faultlessly. It is not karma but the fruit of karma that should be surrendered for the benefit of others, and that karma should be endued by the *sattvic* quality of our mind. This is possible only when we make a sincere effort in directing our mind to travel along the *sattvic* avenue and to avoid traveling on the lower avenues of *tamas* and *rajas*.

These three qualities are termed *gunas*. All our actions, thoughts and motivations are guided by these three *gunas—tamas, rajas* and *sattva*. We can divide all humanity into these three categories. *Sattva* is illumination, light, serenity, tranquility and most often represented by the color white. *Rajas* is characterized by activities and movements full of distractions and dissipation, and its symbolical color is red. *Tamas* is sloth, and inertia, most often symbolized by black and dark blue, the color of darkness. The aspirant should gradually get rid of the actions endued by *tamas* and *rajas* and finally establish his whole life pattern on the basis of *sattva*. By establishing *sattva* and tranquility he purifies his mind, attains emotional maturity and starts meditating on the center of consciousness, which is pure and self-illumined *Atman* in all living beings. It is never *Atman* that is impure, but the mind which remains covered with the dust of ignorance. The *samskaras* form dust on the mirror of the mind. The soul cannot be seen in the mirror when the mind remains covered with dust. It is *tamasic* and *rajasic* actions and thoughts that form this heavy film on the surface of the mirror called mind. Through constant self-purification by maintaining awareness in performing our actions in the external world, doing our duties selflessly and not having desires for pleasure, we will be able to cleanse our minds and thus see the reflection of soul in the mirror of mind.

If we see a stick half in and half out of water, it appears to have a broken shape. In the same manner our thinking process does not allow us to see the true nature of our soul, and unless the waves of the stream of the thinking force are calmed we cannot realize the correct view of the soul. Meditation helps in calming down that disturbed thinking process and helps in revealing the soul. In higher states of meditation the aspirant pierces the delusion of *maya* and goes beyond. This is the goal of human life.

6

Attachment
and Non-Attachment

We must learn how to live our lives to facilitate the process of liberation. We should always accept life as a challenge and not be disappointed by anything, for life is simply a vehicle for us. Sooner or later we will find God or Truth within ourselves. We will realize that we do not exist as individual entities. It is only our ignorance that makes us think that we exist apart from the whole. We need to replace manhood by Godhood, and for this we must become real human beings. We need to realize that we are ancient travelers in this world and that our purpose is to attain perfection.

In the West there is a widespread fear of losing the ego or personality. Through meditation we find that we can expand the ego, not lose it. We must become large-hearted. We must take in more and more of our fellow beings and the rest of the world rather than identify with the individual, isolated self. We must think of ourselves as travelers temporarily passing through life in this world. We must realize that we are only using this body, these experiences, these material objects temporarily on loan. They are not ours. We are borrowing them. Sooner or later we will leave them behind. There is nothing to fear; our purpose is not to possess these things but to use them in order to transcend them. This is the truth which goes beyond the law. It is in this sense that Jesus' Sermon on the Mount goes beyond Moses' law for those disciples who are ready. We must learn that our actions are not our personal possessions. We need not be attached to them.

It is of utmost importance to understand the principle of detachment in order to become free from the fruits of our actions. Detachment, or better, non-attachment, does not mean non-enjoyment. Normally when we perform an action we are not free from the fruits of that action. For example, when we pray we usually ask for something. This is known as *man-centered* prayer in which demands are made. Even though we are praying this is not a liberating act for we are attached to the fruits of our prayer. There is another kind of prayer called *God-centered* which is for the purpose of enlightenment. Examples are "Lord, help me in en-lightening myself," or "Help me to attain freedom." However, even in these cases, to consider God outside of ourselves does not help us. It is more important to think that God is within us so that we see ourselves as an instrument, a son, a servant of the Beloved, of God. In this way we may approach a prayer as an act of non-attachment.

You may always choose the relationship with God which best suits you. If He is your friend, then you may accept His guidance. If you recognize Him as your guide, then you may know yourself as His instrument. You must have confidence that God is within you. Friends make you lonely because they lead you to seek help from the external world. In order to achieve understanding and self-knowledge through non-attachment you need meditation. Meditation enables you to perfect yourself all alone. All alone means "all in one." It does not mean lonely. People make you lonely. Only your friend within can help you. Fulfillment comes only from within. Other people can give you help but not fulfillment. There is no point in demanding love either. By giving love you will receive love in return, but still no one can satisfy you. You alone can satisfy yourself through the Supreme *I*. Through meditation you can allow your *I* to meet the Supreme *I*.

It is the rope of karma which binds us and prevents us from realizing this. There are two paths to achieve liberation from this bondage. They are (1) renunciation, and (2) non-attachment. On the first path we say, "I don't want any pleasure which is not practical in helping me achieve my goal. Thus I choose to lead a monastic life." This is a path for very few. It is a razor's edge. On the second path we learn to live in the world but to do our actions properly. It is this second path we are going to study, the method of non-attachment.

Normally we are slaves of our duties. We become attached to our activities and their consequences and thereby plunge further into bondage. If you do something purely out of a sense of duty, then you will understand nothing and make no progress. If you fulfill a desire for your husband or wife out of duty toward him or her, then you will be attached either through resentment or guilt or annoyance or some other kind of disturbing emotion. If your duties and actions are not "oiled" with love you are creating greater bondage for yourself. If you perform your actions out of love, then you are doing them selflessly. This is very easy to understand, for if I do something selflessly for you, then you, not I, will receive the fruits of my action. Learn to do your actions for humanity and to let humanity reap the fruits. This is the way to become free through non-attachment.

Tyagi is the Sanskrit term for one who renounces the fruits of his actions, not the actions themselves. In this world you must do your actions, but you must do them selflessly and skillfully. Non-attachment does not mean not to love, and it also does not mean indifference and aloofness. Rather it means to act with love. You should not disturb your life and your mind with attached selfish acts. Life is too short for that. As it is, we spend most of our lives eating, sleeping, talking and going to the bathroom. We must learn to take life lightly but also to do our duty seriously with love, skill and selflessness.

It is not the action itself which binds us but the fruits of that action. Action, like a policeman, arrests but does not punish us—the fruits of our actions punish us. Desire is motivated by the fruits of our actions. Do not try to preserve and protect the fruits of your actions by coveting them. Ail qualities, such as jealousy, hatred and pride come to you in this way.

We should not seek satisfaction in life but rather *santosha* or contentment. It is the inability to achieve satisfaction in life which finally motivates us to seek liberation. We are, in fact, passing through a phase of dutiful actions to be performed in this life. We cannot live without doing these actions, but by doing them selflessly, skillfully, and lovingly we can avoid becoming attached to them. This does not mean indifference, for that is mere escapism. We seek escape from our problems when we cannot cope with them. Non-attachment means doing our actions in equilibrium and tranquility, especially when we are offered the fruits of these actions. This is the real trial, for we bind ourselves either when we receive the fruits of our actions or when we are denied them. Through non-attachment we learn that the true enjoyment of the fruits of our actions comes only when we offer them to God or to humanity. The Upanishads teach that actions which are helpful in the path of liberation should never be renounced.

Understand the meaning of life. Eating, sleeping and other natural functions, without an understanding of the purpose of life, makes an animal of man. To be a human being, one needs to know the purpose of life. That purpose is liberation, and liberation can be achieved through non-attached actions. Any obstacle in life can also become a means to liberation. Whatever gives you pain can also give you liberating knowledge. It is not the objects of the world but our attitude toward them which gives us pleasure and pain. The Sanskrit word, *dvandvas* means "pairs of inseparable opposites." It matters little whether we derive pleasure or pain from an experience; both are equally binding and both are present in varying amounts in all our experiences. In life we must learn to transform all things which give us pleasure and pain; we must learn to use them to help us in our spiritual progress, not to become disturbed by either.

In order to transform these disturbances we need patience. Unfortunately in the West patience is sorely lacking. Patience can transform any obstacle into a vehicle. The same breeze which disturbs and puts out a small flame can also turn that small flame into a forest fire.

Nishkamakarma in Sanskrit means "selfless, skillful. desireless love." It is through *nishkamakarma* that we can transform obstacles and become free from the rope of karma. It is by not fleeing from our actions that we can achieve this. We may seek a monastic life only after we have perfected our self-analysis. We must study ourselves, using our own faculties of discrimination and wisdom. We must learn the reasons for our dissatisfaction with the present known circumstances and for our fear of future unknown circumstances. We must not seek to escape or avoid our actions and duties in this life. When we perform acts for others we are in fact worshipping God in a concrete sense. It is God, not man, who comes first in karma.

Nor should we seek transcendence too quickly. We must first learn how to do our actions before we go beyond them. It is through non-attached actions that we prepare ourselves for knowledge and truth in the form of grace. *Kripa* is the Sanskrit word for kindness or a kind act coming from above; but *kripa* comes for what you have done. It does not come for nothing and free of charge. John received the revelation because of what he had achieved through his long practice of meditation. He was not simply chosen at random. After you have done your work skillfully, grace will come to you. Grace is not an exception to the law; it follows the law. If you find the heat of the sun is oppressive, you might wish for a miracle of shade; but it will not be forthcoming. If, however, you work diligently and patiently you may nurse a tree until it is large enough to provide the desired shade. The shade may seem like a miracle to others, but you know that it followed only after proper preparation. It is the way with grace. By following the law skillfully you can eventually become free from the bonds of law. All of this comes through non-attachment which means love, not indifference. By following the path of non-attachment life becomes a song, a poem. For this we need patience and courage.

Let us take our example from the sages. A sage is like a tree laden with fruit. If you throw a stone at it, it gives you fruit. No matter what you do to a sage, his response will give you sustenance and will help you. On the other hand, you must guard against a bad man, because he can harm you. When a sage becomes angry with you it is out of love, and his anger will be seen as a vehicle for your progress. Learn to welcome the disturbances which seem to come to you as obstacles. Learn to transform them with patience and courage. Then all of the experiences of your life will seem to you as the responses of a sage who is providing vehicles for your progress.

What is really necessary for examining the trials of life and attaining freedom? A sixteenth-century sage by the name of Tulsidasa noted four points to examine in time of need: religion, friendship, patience and courage. When an obstacle seems to overcome you, see which of these four will really come to your aid. Your religion or beliefs will fail you, your friends will not be at hand, but your patience and your own courage can come to your aid. They are your best friends.

If your desires are not met, consider that there might be a good reason for it. Be patient. Have the courage to rely on yourself and to practice non-attachment. Have the courage to doubt your own doubts before doubting others, to recognize these doubts as the negative parts of your own mind. Act skillfully with love, patience and courage and recall that love harbors no expectations from others. Doing something selflessly for others is true love. To do your duty with love is to be like the lotus that remains unsoiled by the mud in which it grows. Learn to live in this world yet to be above it. Learn that everything in this world is meant for you to use but never to possess.

7

Mind and Mantra

Why do we need a *mantra,* how does it help us? A mantra is a unique word or phrase which when properly understood and correctly used will liberate your mind from all agonies, whether these are physical, mental or spiritual in origin. It is mind that stands as a wall between you and reality, for mind normally is in a diffused, dissipated condition.

Mantra is a Sanskrit word which is derived from the root *man,* "to think," (in Greek *menos,* in Latin *mens)* and is combined with *tra* which stands for liberation, thus meaning that which helps in liberating mind from bondage and misery. Mantra creates a mental image and is a transcending power which leads to the silence of omnipresence.

"In the beginning was the Word, and the Word was with God and the Word was God . . . the Word was made flesh."

Word comes from its origin of force and reality. The source of mantra was discovered by the great sages while experiencing a specific state known as the superconscious state. When related to the source, a word carries a meaning, a feeling, and a purpose. A mere sound prescribed by an ordinary teacher cannot lead the student to higher states of enlightenment. It may help engage the mind consciously or unconciously and as a result lead to feelings of relaxation. However, the sound alone cannot lead one to the other shore of life. Meaning, feeling and purpose must all be part of mantra practice if such a destination is to be reached. Moreover the mantra must be coordinated with other yogic purification practices if it is to attain full potency.

Mantras can only be effective when the mind is purified. This long tradition is an expression of the highest knowledge and experience in the realm of human psychology, though this experience is acquired by the guidance of a guru and by constant practice of the mantra. The secret of the correct use of a mantra is to coordinate its practice with a life of self-discipline and purity. The mantra reveals its potential more and more when it is assimilated into the deeper levels of one's being. It leads one from the surface to the deeper realms and finally to the highest state. The ancient science of mantra is an expression of man's highest knowledge and experience in the realm of human psychology. The ordinary man who is not acquainted with the theories and laboratory practices cannot understand what that science is about. Similarly, without the guidance of a guru and actual experience with a mantra, no real grasp of the potential of this discipline is possible. When a mantra is used with the help of a competent teacher it becomes a means for making the mind one-pointed and tranquil.

Generally we have some person in our lives to whom we can turn for help—a teacher, a psychiatrist, a wife, a friend.

There are times, however, when no one can help us. For example, between death and rebirth there is an intermediate period in which we have no tongue to talk with and no body to use. The conscious mind slowly fails, and the subconscious mind which has stored up our merits and demerits becomes more active. The conscious mind is a small part of the whole. The subconscious mind is a vast storehouse of experiences, memories, emotions, fears, fantasies and images. During the period between death and rebirth the subconscious mind dominates our mental experiences and reveals its vast store of images and fantasies to us. At this time there is no one to help us, no friend or counsel, and it is then that a mantra can come to our aid. During our embodied life, as we repeat our mantra, the subconscious mind slowly stores it away and brings it forth later during times of trial or difficulty to help and guide us. During the period after death and before rebirth our mantra may help us overcome the images of our subconscious mind and prevent us from being overwhelmed by them. The mantra can guide us through this difficult period as no friend or teacher can.

In the process of meditation we must learn to explore our minds so that the mantra may be used effectively. The first stage of meditation is to clear the mind. We all know that we think but do not know why or what are the root causes of our thoughts. It is essential to observe the thinking process and witness the contents of our minds. To establish ourselves in our own basic nature we need to know how to cleanse the mind. Normally we present ourselves well before others, but the problem is that we do not know how to make a good presentation to ourselves. We constantly identify with the content of the mind and with our memories. Things which trouble us inwardly are hidden from others, but we see them and allow ourselves to be disturbed constantly by them. Through meditation we gain control over these disturbances and learn to observe and witness them. Then slowly problems fade from our mental processes.

There is a bed of memory in the mind where we store the seeds of our impressions or *samskaras*. Without this bed the river of mind cannot flow. From this bed arise many of the memories and impressions which trouble and disturb us. In meditation we learn first to calm down the conscious mind so that these impressions may be allowed to rise and pass through our mind without troubling us. Then we learn to deal with the deeper memories of the subconscious mind with which we normally have no contact. In our educational system we learn only to train the conscious mind, but in meditation we deal with the whole mind. When the conscious mind has been calmed we learn to integrate all the parts of the mind and to bring them to a single point of concentration. This is known as making the mind one-pointed.

The conscious mind is used in the waking state. We do not have total control over the conscious mind. Sometimes it sleeps, and we become "absent-minded." This is why meditation is of such great value. By mental and silent repetition of the mantra and in engaging in internal "dialogues" which help us to analyze our inner selves, we may slowly develop *sankalpa,* i.e., unconscious determination or resolve. *Sankalpa* helps us slowly to gain control over the conscious mind, to calm it down and eventually to bring the other parts of the mind and the other states of consiousness within our awareness.

Human beings normally experience three states of consciousness as we have already mentioned: waking, dreaming and sleeping. The great sages of the past found it necessary to go to a fourth state of consciousness, the state of sleepless sleep, *samadhi.* In this fourth state we find tranquility. It is to achieve this tranquility that one practices meditation. We slowly learn not to be disturbed when the mind interferes during meditation. We must learn simply to observe the disturbing thoughts and let them pass. For this we need patience, and we need to inspect our thinking process. We must recall that what is going on in our minds is produced by us. We should inspect it and always recognize it as our own product. Each person's thinking is his own creation. It will not help to project our thoughts onto others and to blame them for the things which trouble us; nor will it help to allow things we did five years ago to trouble us today for they are not our present actions. Brooding does not help. We should let the bubbles which arise from the depths of the pool of the mind vanish slowly. Do not fight with your thoughts for this will only interfere with your meditation even more. Simply observe things and watch them as a calm witness. Meditate; do not fight with your thoughts.

We begin by learning to inspect and analyze our own minds. First we find that we do indeed have minds because we think. We come to realize that we are not the same as our thinking process and our minds. Through analysis, through introspection we learn to discriminate between the thinker and the thinking process. You can say to yourself, "My body is different from me; my senses are different from me; my mind is different from me. These things are like garments which I wear. I may cast off these garments, but I will never lose my identity." You may lose many things, but you will never lose your own Self. You always remain aware of the *I* which you can distinguish from the *I* that is doing and thinking. If you have no self-control, you are simply a slave. The first step to control and liberation is self-observation.

When you observe yourself you find that there is a mental "train" which is constantly running through your mind. This train contains symbols, ideas, imaginings, fantasies and fancies. We tend to identify with these things, to feel that they are part of us and yet to know that in some basic way they are of a different order of reality. We know that there is something in us, an identity which is distinct and separate from all of our mental objects. We realize this especially when we cannot see or feel; when our senses are cut off, we still have a sense of identity, a sense of self. It is that self which must be pursued deeper and deeper, separating it from all other experiences. We may watch the train, but we must not identify with it. Recall that the train is simply our own product. There is no need to fear anything in this train of thought because we love ourselves. The inner Self remains tranquil above all of the experiences and objects of this mental train. Fear means "no love"; fearless means "full of love." So it is love for ourselves, this inner identity, which will allow us to remain tranquil and transcend the experiences of our mind.

Anything that comes into our mind belongs to one of the categories of objects in the mental train. We need only to observe them. Even though it is not clear where the train comes from or where it will go, simply observe it and let it pass. Never suppress or struggle with your feelings. Never hold back your desires or try to argue. Simply analyze them, inspect them, let them all pass. Never identify with them.

Of course this analysis should be done mentally. It is not necessary to express your feelings and desires openly or in acts. Simply analyze, observe and witness them during self-examination. When new symbols arise in the mind, observe them and persist in remembering your mantra. If the mind train lingers on and refuses to go away, simply watch it. Stand there and watch the train go by.

This process of purifying, cleansing and emptying the mind is absolutely essential for successful meditation. We must not seek too quickly and impatiently to achieve higher states and higher experiences before we have managed to empty the mind from disturbing thoughts and to calm it. In a monastery novices do not begin with meditation. First students are taught to purify their minds. Modem man is too impatient and wants to master the art of meditation immediately.

Learn to have a dialogue between the observer and that which is being observed. Follow the imagination in this dialogue, analyze and observe the train of mental objects, and slowly control will be gained over these things. We rise above them, and they disappear from the domain of mind.

Never meditate after having just eaten a meal, when rushed or when angry, for these conditions occupy the mind and prevent proper observation of the thinking process. Too often in meditation the mind is occupied, and if the mind is not free then we are not free. If we cannot learn to go beyond the thinking process, examine it. Slowly become aware of the separation between *you* and *your thoughts*. Thoughts will appear and disappear, but always learn to be a witness. Do not identify with thoughts, images and symbols. In this way we will learn which of our thinking processes are helpful and which are harmful. Always recall that our train of thoughts is our own product; it is our own direct creation and that is why it affects us.

It is at this point in meditation training that a mantra becomes invaluable. The mantra is like a seed, and we are like the soil. The mantra needs time to grow. The mantra must be nourished. Persevere in repeating it mentally and silently within and slowly a new object will grow and come to occupy the mind. Eventually instead of watching our thoughts we will begin to watch ourselves repeating our mantra. The stages in the learning process are these: introspection, observation, witnessing and liberation. Good and bad thoughts will cease to have meaning when we stop identifying with them. We will see that these are merely mental objects for us to observe and witness. We will find that that which is already realized and which never changes is the Self, and that which changes, grows and decays is non-Self. As meditation progresses we will separate these two and identify more strongly with the Self and less with the non-Self. To accomplish this we need only mindful self-analysis and remembering of our mantra.

8

Liberation
and Selfless Action

Knowledge alone liberates. As a blazing fire reduces a pile of wood to ashes, so the fire of wisdom reduces all actions to ashes, says the Gita. Wisdom or knowledge does not nullify actions, only their binding power. Wisdom and knowledge purify the way of life and action. A rope can bind no more when it is burned, though it may still appear as a rope of bondage. Similarly actions bind man, but if they have been tempered by the fire of wisdom they may retain the appearance of action but will no longer have the power to bind. The energy that finds expression in the action has been transformed into knowledge and wisdom.

How are we to create in us that fire of knowledge in which to burn the *samskaras* which motivate our actions? We cannot escape our actions by trying to run away from them. Closing our eyes or running away from an action does not make it vanish. It will still be there when we open our eyes again. Life's problems are not to be avoided. They have to be faced and accepted. Coming to grips with life and karma by meeting their challenges with knowledge, spiritual strength and skillful action done selflessly is the only way to be free from karma. Very often people believe in doing good and adopt it as a philosophy of life. This cannot go very far if it is only an outward expression. Belief only in what one considers good is a superficial philosophy. It proves inadequate when confronted by the trials of life. The greatest strength comes only from a deep selflessness in life, and that is expressed through mind, action and speech. One must not forget that the source of this strength is *Atman*, the very soul of oneself. After careful self-examination, having pondered the meaning and significance of life, one must try to live performing actions selflessly to the last breath of one's life. Inaction leads to inertia, and selfish actions can become a bondage which tightens the rope of karma.

Selfishness is the negation of spiritual awareness. Animals are meant to be selfish for they have no experience of their true selves. The world of objects comprises their sole sphere of awareness. It is only in human beings that subjective awareness is found. Control and discipline and knowing the art of doing one's actions in harmony with one's psycho-physical personality are means for man to deepen his self-awareness and realize himself as pure *Atman*, the eternal self-illumined, ever-free Self. Trying to save or protect one's physical existence in the external world is to commit spiritual suicide by losing the opportunity to unfold one's being-state in its totality.

What we call fate is also man's making. That which is done by man in the past becomes his fate. By knowing the art of living and by acting selflessly we can go beyond time, space and causality. The human mind defines objects and events of the world of experience in terms of space and time. What exactly is space and time? They have no absolute reality in themselves. They are only relative concepts. When the mind is made one-pointed it moves to a higher dimension of awareness where there is no time, space or causality, and there freedom from *samskaras* becomes possible.

Grief and delusion come as a result of self-identification with limited physical and mental states. Identifying with the body, senses and mind, which are only minor dimensions of our being, we remain weak, helpless and limited, cut off from others. In such a state of weakness we make all sorts of mistakes which reinforce the rope of karma and add to the *samskaras* that commit us to endless rounds of births and deaths.

Lacking awareness of the Truth within us, we separate ourselves from the whole and thus create a small personality, a personal mask for ourselves. Selfless actions done to the best of one's ability lead to a state of tranquility. It is only a tranquil mind that can experience all levels of consciousness and finally attain liberation.

Samskaras can also be seen as the consequences of the primary sin of ignorance which cuts us off from the mainstream of life. A river cut off from its mainstream becomes stagnant; the man cut off from the mainstream of life degenerates and falls into grief and delusion.

The capacity of awareness grows in the human mind by the disciplined practicing of social awareness as a citizen and by following an inner discipline as a spiritual seeker. Total discipline helps man in achieving freedom from all cords, gross and subtle, of karma and *samskaras*. When one learns how to perform selfless actions, one simultaneously expands the mind and goes to transpersonal levels of mind. This leads to an awakening to the basic unity of existence and consequently to liberation. Thus by doing one's duty selflessly one is practicing spirituality in daily life.

When equality and diversity does not remain an unsolved riddle in the human mind, then salvation will be possible. There will always be differences of opinion regarding what is the best karma, but such differences will only be on the surface. Deep down there is only one unity. Whatever work or action man does, whatever his position in life, he contains within himself an integral value, the spiritual value proceeding from his soul. When man learns to spiritualize his actions, thoughts and desires he will be able to perform actions and duties without bondage. Then the subtle traces of *samskaras* will not germinate at all.

Thus when we want to avoid the sufferings and sorrows arising from *samskaras* we should discipline our senses, organs of action and mind at all levels but be careful not to ignore our duties.

Man pays his karmic debts only by performing selfless actions. Without paying our karmic debts to the people with whom we live, for example, or to the family into which we are born, we will have no way of attaining freedom. So it is absolutely necessary for one to discharge one's duties and thus to remain free from the obligations of karmic debts.

Actually we choose our parents and they choose us. Like attracts like. Working to perform our duties conscientiously and sincerely among the people with whom we live helps us in not creating further bondages and obstacles in the path of enlightenment. The fire of knowledge burns on the fuel of selfless actions, and thus karmic debts are met. To gain freedom from past actions and karmas one should learn to act so that

karma becomes a useful tool rather than an obstacle on the path
to enlightenment.

The knower, the known and the process of knowing com-
prise the three-fold nature of the drive to action. Instrument,
activity and event are the three-fold components that accomplish action. Each of these three divisions is in accordance with
the three qualities of *sattva, rajas* and *tamas.* The universe contains many beings. Each being is unique. Variety is the nature
of the universe. In this diversity one feels the presence of one-
ness-, this is due to *sattva*-endued knowledge. The site of the
undivided reality in diversity is known because of *sattva.* For
example, the ocean has many waves and they are distinct from
one another, yet they are all made from the same water. To see
the same water in different waves is *sattva*-endued knowledge.
Gold is made into various ornaments, but the presence of gold
is common to them all. To see this oneness in different forms is
*sattva-e*ndued knowledge. There exist in the world many religious faiths—Hinduism, Buddhism, Christianity, Judaism, etc.
Yet in spite of this multiplicity, one can see in them all a oneness of being and can accordingly relate in one way towards all
of them. This results from *sattva*-endued knowledge. Human
beings, birds, beasts and insects are all different, yet they possess the one life principle in common. To regard them all as
alike is due to sattva-endued knowledge alone.

Rajas-endued knowledge enables one to realize division
and variety of forms. The variety of aspects in each object is
seen by *rajas*-endued knowledge. This sort of disposition which
fastens on diversity alone is due to *rajas.* It frustrates all efforts
towards seeing unity in diversity.

Tamas-endued knowledge actually obscures the relation of
cause and effect and is completely unable to reveal Truth. It is the

cause of attachment to a part as if it were the whole. It is the cause of ignorance which confuses cause and effect. It is false knowledge, sheer ignorance and impure ideas and is contrary to enlightenment. This is the defect of tamas-endued knowledge. *Tamas*-endued people take a part for the whole and attach themselves to that part. They even lead themselves to destroy the whole. This level of knowledge leads to destruction and attachment.

Thus *sattva*-endued knowledge sees unity in diversity while tamas-endued knowledge sees diversity even in unity. Sattva-endued knowledge inspires one to perform actions with the goal of self-realization while *tamas*-endued knowledge leads to self-degradation. That action is called *sattvic-endued* which is done without attachment, without lust or hatred and without a selfish desire to enjoy the fruit of one's own actions. Lust and hatred make the mind waver and pleasure leads to self-enjoyment. They all make the mind extremely agitated. They must be renounced if one is to pursue the tranquil mind.

An action that is done with a tranquil mind is a *sattvic* action; but an action that is done with the desire to selfishly enjoy the fruit, with a view always to keep it for one's own enjoyment, ignoring its cost in labor and effort and with overwhelming confidence in one's ability, that action is *rajasic. Sattvic* actions are performed without egoism, without thought of enjoying the fruits, without attachment, lust or hatred. *Rajasic* actions are permeated with all of these negative qualities. Actions done without the desire to enjoy their fruits will undoubtedly lead to greater happiness. *Rajasic* actions can lead only to greater misery. *Tamasic* action leads only to degradation. It happens without thought of what damage or injury it might cause. Therefore, one should observe oneself carefully to guard against performing *tamasic* actions.

The type of actions a person commits is determined by his disposition. One whose steadiness of mind remains undisturbed in doing actions and duties is indeed a balanced man. He who is not elated with success or disappointed with failure is a *sattvic* man. Such a man possesses courage. No anxieties about success or failures worry him. He is neither puffed up with success nor downhearted with failure.

The characteristic of a *rajasic* man is that he is given to enjoyment. He has a keen desire for pleasure. At the root of all his activities lies the drive for enjoyment. He naturally seeks enjoyment from the fruits of his own action. He who is attached to pleasure is bound to be greedy. Having gotten some pleasure, he yearns for more pleasure; having lost them, his grief is beyond description. Joy and grief swing his mind one way or the other. Thus he is perpetually agitated. Such a restless man finds it difficult to really enjoy any pleasure. On the spur of the moment he can become violent; especially if he confronts any obstacle in the way of his enjoyment, he may even react and try to destroy it. This increases the hatred and violence in a *rajasic* man. Violence is always accompanied by uncleanliness of body and mind. Where enjoyment, greed and violence dwell it is impossible to maintain the body, speech and mind in serenity.

The characteristics of a *tamasic* man are ignorance and delusion, for he has no competence to do anything skillfully. A *tamasic* man is devoid of good conduct because of his very ignorance; only a man of good conduct can become a good human being. A *tamasic* man is completely devoid of true knowledge. Filled with delusions, he cannot contribute in knowledgeable discussions, nor perform any activity with skill, nor propagate good ideas. He remains lazy and dull in all circumstances. In the absence of inspiration there is no possibility of self-advancement through action, work or duty. When unable to grow through one's own actions, duties and efforts, the mind begins to run in crooked avenues of *tamas,* and one always grieves over failure. Such a man begins to hate others; he never rejoices at other people's success. He is always sad, gloomy and hateful.

Of the various functions of the mind, *buddhi,* or intellect, is the highest. It is *buddhi* which decides, discriminates and judges. This *buddhi* can also be classified into three categories: *sattvic, rajasic* and *tamasic. Sattvic buddhi* correctly and rightly shows to what one should proceed and from what one should keep away, what causes bondage and what dispels the bondage of the aspirant. The *rajasic buddhi* is involved with the selfish motivations only and runs through the avenues of pleasures. The *tamasic buddhi* cannot discriminate between duty and non-duty, bondage and freedom, independence and dependence and always presents false pictures. This deludes the aspirant, he forms a perverse view of things and does not see anything in its true colors at all. A *tamasic* man cannot decide what to do and what not to do.

Pleasures can also be classified as *sattvic, rajasic* and *tamasic.* The *sattvic* pleasures in the beginning seem to be painful, but their results are beneficial in the long run. They bring serenity of mind, knowledge, penance, control of the senses and self-purification, which results purify the way of the soul. *Sattvic* pleasure finds joy everywhere, in all conditions in life, in the control of mind and in self-realization, as well as in doing actions selflessly for the sake of humanity as a worship of God. *Rajasic* pleasure is produced by contact of the senses with their objects. It vanishes when the object vanishes. A *rajasic* man feels pleasure in efforts that obtain pleasure for himself. *Rajasic* pleasure ends painfully.

Tamasic pleasure is pain which produces misery. It increases sleep, laziness and inactivity. A *tamasic* man does not feel like doing anything. He feels pleasure in laziness.

All things that appear on the face of the earth and in the universe are endued with the three qualities of *sattva, rajas* and *tamas.* The whole universe is a play of these three qualities. These qualities are found in the subtle traces of *samskaras* and determine the life course here and hereafter. If anyone wants to examine one's own disposition, he can do so by examining the quality of his mind. If one starts observing himself impartially, he can find out whether his disposition is *sattvic, rajasic* or *tamasic* and thus determine the future course he has to take. He can also find out which rung of the spiritual ladder he stands on.

To attain freedom from the rounds of birth and death and from the bondage of karma one should learn to do his duty whole-heartedly. A man attains perfection and achieves perfect eminence by devotion to his proper work and duty. If he gives up his own duty and does what is not his duty, he cannot rise. The question is: "What is one's duty?"

One's duty is that which is determined by one's inborn qualities or *samskaras.* For instance, if man has the quality of *sattva* in a dormant state he should practice tranquility, control of the senses, etc. If he has *sattva*-dominated *rajas,* his proper duty should be to follow the path of action and practice meditation in action. In this way a man can succeed in doing his duties by studying his inborn qualities or Karma is inevitable; work is worship. By worshipping that Absolute One from whom all beings have sprung and by whom all this universe is pervaded, a man attains right perfection.

The soul is the inner dweller of this body. He who pervades the body and has spread His power into the mind, eyes, ears and other senses is the object of worship of the senses. It is He whom the senses worship by means of their works—the legs by their movement, the arms by their work of protection, the stomach by its work of digestion, the heart by the circulation of blood throughout the body, the mind by contemplating, the intellect by deciding and so on. All the senses and organs are thus always worshipping Him, each in its own particular way. The worship of the soul is carried on within oneself by one's own work. None of these senses gives up its own work and does another's. Each contributes to success by doing its own ordained work well. The power that pervades the whole universe, pervades mankind too. We all are parts of that same Omnipresence. Therefore, it is He whom we serve by our proper work.

It is not possible for anyone to live without doing his own action, duty or karma. Karma is the only way to cleanse the life process, and without cleansing we cannot attain perfection. The universe is the manifestation of the unmanifest eternal Truth. We see a ripple arise and play on the surface of the lake; it lasts for an instant and then disappears. Whence did it come, what was it, and where did it go? From water it came; having come, it is water still, and unto water it returns in the end. The real nature of that momentary existence, the ripple, is water. Similarly, Truth is the real nature of the universe. When one is caught up in the trivial waves of passing sense experience, then one finds change, death, destruction in every phase of life, and no safe structure of life can be erected. When awareness is developed and the eternal is realized in the midst of the non-eternal, then eternal peace dawns.

To see the eternal in the midst of the non-eternal is the purpose of karma yoga. By affirming the eternal and negating the non-eternal we pass to the other shore of life. Affirmation and negation should both be present if we are to enjoy this world. What supports us is not what we renounce, but what we possess. This world is worthy of enjoyment, and we should know the art of enjoying. Before we can enjoy this world we have to learn the correct approach. Duty done out of selfish motives is far inferior to that done with a detached attitude. Petty-minded are they who are motivated by selfishness. They bring upon themselves suffering and misery. Renunciation is an eternal maxim. There cannot be real enjoyment without purification through renunciation. In our lives it is in interpersonal relationships that we derive the greatest joy and not by affirming our little selves. When we deny our little selves through renunciation of selfish motives, desires and attachments, we identify with the Self of all and make contact with real life. Negation leads to a larger affirmation.

Karma teaches us the ethical and spiritual values of life, the art of living and enjoying life. When the mind is yoked to the ultimate good through cultivation of detachment, which is the highest form of love, then one takes delight in loving all and excluding none. Nothing is evil, but without yoking the mind to the soul and cultivating dispassion for the unreal, real compassion is not possible. To develop an ethical nature becomes easy when one starts enjoying and working selflessly for others, and once the habit is formed one cannot live without doing so. By dedicating the fruits of actions and negating the sense of ego, one fulfills the real purpose of life. Without achieving freedom from the spirit of exploitation, one cannot enjoy life. The world around us is nothing but blissful *Atman,* and we are here to enjoy it. It does not appear to us in its profound and true form because we remain caught up in selfish sense enjoyments. Life does not need to be changed; only our attitudes do.

About Swami Rama

ONE OF THE greatest adepts, teachers, writers, and humanitarians of the 20th century, Swami Rama is the founder of the Himalayan Institute. Born in the Himalayas, he was raised from early childhood by the great Himalayan sage, Bengali Baba. Under the guidance of his master he traveled from monastery to monastery and studied with a variety of Himalayan saints and sages, including his grandmaster, who was living in a remote region of Tibet. In addition to this intense spiritual training, Swami Rama received higher education in both India and Europe. From 1949 to 1952, he held the prestigious position of Shankaracharya of Karvirpitham in South India. Thereafter, he returned to his master to receive further training at his cave monastery, and finally, in 1969, came to the United States, where he founded the Himalayan Institute. His best-known work, *Living with the Himalayan Masters*, reveals the many facets of this singular adept and demonstrates his embodiment of the living Himalayan Tradition.

The main building of the Himalayan Institute headquarters near Honesdale, Pennsylvania

The Himalayan Institute

A leader in the field of yoga, meditation, spirituality, and holistic health, the Himalayan Institute is a nonprofit international organization dedicated to serving humanity through educational, spiritual, and humanitarian programs. The mission of the Himalayan Institute is to inspire, educate, and empower all those who seek to experience their full potential.

Founded in 1971 by Swami Rama of the Himalayas, the Himalayan Institute and its varied activities and programs exemplify the spiritual heritage of mankind that unites East and West, spirituality and science, ancient wisdom and modern technology.

Our international headquarters is located on a beautiful 400-acre campus in the rolling hills of the Pocono Mountains of northeastern Pennsylvania. Our spiritually vibrant community and peaceful setting provide the perfect atmosphere for seminars and retreats, residential programs, and holistic health services. Students from all over the world join us to attend diverse programs on subjects such as hatha yoga, meditation, stress reduction, ayurveda, and yoga and tantra philosophy.

In addition, the Himalayan Institute draws on roots in the yoga tradition to serve our members and community through the following programs, services, and products:

Mission Programs

The essence of the Himalayan Institute's teaching mission flows from the timeless message of the Himalayan Masters, and is echoed in our on-site mission programming. Their message is to first become aware of the reality within ourselves, and then to build a bridge between our inner and outer worlds.

Our mission programs express a rich body of experiential wisdom and are offered year-round. They include seminars, retreats, and professional certifications that bring you the best of an authentic yoga tradition, addressed to a modern audience. Join us on campus for our Mission Programs to find wisdom from the heart of the yoga tradition, guidance for authentic practice, and food for your soul.

Wisdom Library and Mission Membership

The Himalayan Institute online Wisdom Library curates the essential teachings of the living Himalayan Tradition. This offering is a unique counterpart to our in-person Mission Programs, empowering students by providing online learning resources to enrich their study and practice outside the classroom.

Our Wisdom Library features multimedia blog content, livestreams, podcasts, downloadable practice resources, digital courses, and an interactive Seeker's Forum. These teachings capture our Mission Faculty's decades of study, practice, and teaching experience, featuring new content as well as the timeless teachings of Swami Rama and Pandit Rajmani Tigunait.

We invite seekers and students of the Himalayan Tradition to become a Himalayan Institute Mission Member, which grants unlimited access to the Wisdom Library. Mission Membership offers a way for you to support our shared commitment to service, while deepening your study and practice in the living Himalayan Tradition.

Spiritual Excursions

Since 1972, the Himalayan Institute has been organizing pilgrimages for spiritual seekers from around the world. Our spiritual excursions follow the traditional pilgrimage routes where adepts of the Himalayas lived and practiced. For thousands of years, pilgrimage has been an essential part of yoga sadhana, offering spiritual seekers the opportunity to experience the transformative power of living shrines of the Himalayan Tradition.

Global Humanitarian Projects

The Himalayan Institute's humanitarian mission is yoga in action—offering spiritually grounded healing and transformation to the world. Our humanitarian projects serve impoverished communities in India, Mexico, and Cameroon through rural empowerment and environmental regeneration. By putting yoga philosophy into practice, our programs are empowering communities globally with the knowledge and tools needed for a lasting social transformation at the grassroots level.

Publications

The Himalayan Institute publishes over 60 titles on yoga, philosophy, spirituality, science, ayurveda, and holistic health. These include the best-selling books *Living with the Himalayan Masters* and *The Science of Breath*, by Swami Rama; *The Power of Mantra and the Mystery of Initiation, From Death to Birth, Tantra Unveiled,* and two commentaries on the *Yoga Sutra—The Secret of the Yoga Sutra: Samadhi Pada* and *The Practice of the Yoga Sutra: Sadhana Pada*— by Pandit Rajmani Tigunait, PhD; and the award-winning *Yoga: Mastering the Basics* by Sandra Anderson and Rolf Sovik, PsyD. These books are for everyone: the interested reader, the spiritual novice, and the experienced practitioner.

PureRejuv Wellness Center

For over 40 years, the PureRejuv Wellness Center has fulfilled part of the Institute's mission to promote healthy and sustainable lifestyles. PureRejuv combines Eastern philosophy and Western medicine in an integrated approach to holistic health—nurturing balance and healing at home and at work. We offer the opportunity to find healing and renewal through on-site wellness retreats and individual wellness services, including therapeutic massage and bodywork, yoga therapy, ayurveda, biofeedback, natural medicine, and one-on-one consultations with our integrative medical staff.

Total Health Products

The Himalayan Institute, the developer of the original Neti Pot, manufactures a health line specializing in traditional and modern ayurvedic supplements and body care. We are dedicated to holistic and natural living by providing products using non-GMO components, petroleum-free biodegrading plastics, and eco-friendly packaging that has the least impact on the environment. Part of every purchase supports our Global Humanitarian projects, further developing and reinforcing our core mission of spirituality in action.

For further information about our programs, humanitarian projects, and products:

call: 800.822.4547
e-mail: info@HimalayanInstitute.org
write: The Himalayan Institute
           952 Bethany Turnpike
           Honesdale, PA 18431
or visit: HimalayanInstitute.org

HIMALAYAN INSTITUTE®

inherit the wisdom of a living tradition today!

As a Mission Member, you will gain exclusive access to our online Wisdom Library. The Wisdom Library includes monthly livestream workshops, digital practicums and eCourses, monthly podcasts with Himalayan Institute Mission Faculty, and multimedia practice resources.

Wisdom Library

Netra Tantra: Harnessing the Healing Force (Part 1)
Pandit Rajmani Tigunait, PhD | September 28, 2017
Read more

Mission Membership Benefits

- **Never-before-seen content from Swami Rama & Pandit Tigunait**
- **New content announcements & weekly blog roundup**
- **Unlimited access to online yoga classes and meditation classes**
- **Members only digital workshops and monthly livestreams**
- **Downloadable practice resources and Prayers of the Tradition**

Get FREE access to the Wisdom Library for 30 days!

Mission Membership is an invitation to put your spiritual values into action by supporting our shared commitment to service while deepening your study and practice in the living Himalayan Tradition.

BECOME A MISSION MEMBER AT:
himalayaninstitute.org/mission-membership/

The Secret of the Yoga Sutra
Samadhi Pada
Pandit Rajmani Tigunait, PhD

The Yoga Sutra is the living source wisdom of the yoga tradition, and is as relevant today as it was 2,200 years ago when
it was codified by the sage Patanjali. Using this ancient yogic
text as a guide, we can unlock the hidden power of yoga, and
experience the promise of yoga in our lives. By applying its living wisdom in our practice, we can achieve the purpose of life:
lasting fulfillment and ultimate freedom.

Paperback, 6" x 9", 331 pages
$24.95, ISBN 978-0-89389-277-7

The Practice of the Yoga Sutra
Sadhana Pada
Pandit Rajmani Tigunait, PhD

In Pandit Tigunait's practitioner-oriented commentary series,
we see this ancient text through the filter of scholarly understanding and experiential knowledge gained through decades
of advanced yogic practices. Through *The Secret of the Yoga
Sutra* and *The Practice of the Yoga Sutra*, we receive the gift of
living wisdom he received from the masters of the Himalayan
Tradition, leading us to lasting happiness.

Paperback, 6" x 9", 389 Pages
$24.95, ISBN 978-0-89389-279-1

To order: 800-822-4547
Email: mailorder@HimalayanInstitute.org
Visit: HimalayanInstitute.org

Touched by Fire
Pandit Rajmani Tigunait, PhD

This vivid autobiography of a remarkable spiritual leader—
Pandit Rajmani Tigunait, PhD—reveals his experiences and
encounters with numerous teachers, sages, and his master, the
late Swami Rama of the Himalayas. His well-told journey is
filled with years of disciplined study and the struggle to master
the lessons and skills passed to him. *Touched by Fire* brings
Western culture a glimpse of Eastern philosophies in a clear,
understandable fashion, and provides numerous photographs
showing a part of the world many will never see for themselves.

Paperback with flaps, 6" x 9", 296 pages
$16.95, ISBN 978-0-89389-239-5

At the Eleventh Hour
Pandit Rajmani Tigunait, PhD

This book is more than the biography of a great sage—it is a
revelation of the many astonishing accomplishments Swami
Rama achieved in his life. These pages serve as a guide to the
more esoteric and advanced practices of yoga and tantra not
commonly taught or understood in the West. And they bring
you to holy places in India, revealing why these sacred sites are
important and how to go about visiting them. The wisdom in
these stories penetrates beyond the power of words.

Paperback with flaps, 6" x 9", 448 pages
$18.95, ISBN 978-0-89389-211-1

To order: 800-822-4547
Email: mailorder@HimalayanInstitute.org
Visit: HimalayanInstitute.org

Perennial Psychology of the Bhagavad Gita
Swami Rama

With the guidance and commentary of Himalayan Master Swami Rama, you can explore the wisdom of the Bhagavad Gita, which allows one to be vibrant and creative in the external world while maintaining a state of inner tranquility. This commentary on the Bhagavad Gita is a unique opportunity to see the Gita through the perspective of a master yogi, and is an excellent version for practitioners of yoga meditation. Spiritual seekers, psychotherapists, and students of Eastern studies will all find a storehouse of wisdom in this volume.

Paperback, 6" x 9", 479 pages
$19.95, ISBN 978-0-89389-090-2

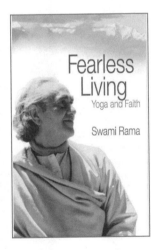

Fearless Living: Yoga and Faith
Swami Rama

Learn to live without fear—to trust a higher power, a divine purpose. In this collection of anecdotes from the astonishing life of Swami Rama, you will understand that there is a way to move beyond mere faith and into the realm of personal revelation. Through his astonishing life experiences we learn about ego and humility, see how to overcome fears that inhibit us, discover sacred places and rituals, and learn the importance of a one-pointed, positive mind. Swami Rama teaches us to see with the eyes of faith and move beyond our self-imposed limitations.

Paperback with flaps, 6" x 9", 160 pages
$12.95, ISBN 978-0-89389-251-7

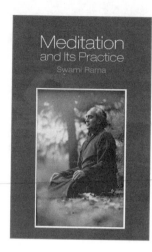

Meditation and Its Practice
Swami Rama

In this practical guide to inner life, Swami Rama teaches us how to slip away from the mental turbulence of our ordinary thought processes into an infinite reservoir of consciousness. This clear, concise meditation manual provides systematic guidance in the techniques of meditation - a powerful tool for transforming our lives and increasing our experience of peace, joy, creativity, and inner tranquility.

Paperback, 6" x 9", 128 pages
$12.95, ISBN 978-0-89389-153-4

The Art of Joyful Living
Swami Rama

In *The Art of Joyful Living*, Swami Rama imparts a message of inspiration and optimism: that you are responsible for making your life happy and emanating that happiness to others. This book shows you how to maintain a joyful view of life even in difficult times.

It contains sections on transforming habit patterns, working with negative emotions, developing strength and willpower, developing intuition, spirituality in loving relationships, learning to be your own therapist, understanding the process of meditation, and more!

Paperback, 6" x 9", 198 pages
$15.95, ISBN 978-0-89389-236-4

To order: 800-822-4547
Email: mailorder@HimalayanInstitute.org
Visit: HimalayanInstitute.org

Tantra Unveiled
Pandit Rajmani Tigunait, PhD

This powerful book describes authentic tantra, what distinguishes it from other spiritual paths, and how the tantric way combines hatha yoga, meditation, visualization, ayurveda, and other disciplines. Taking us back to ancient times, Pandit Tigunait shares his experiences with tantric masters and the techniques they taught him. *Tantra Unveiled* is most valuable for those who wish to live the essence of tantra—practicing spirituality while experiencing a rich outer life.

Paperback, 6" x 9", 152 pages
$14.95, ISBN 978-0-89389-158-9

Moving Inward
Rolf Sovik, PsyD

Rolf Sovik shows readers of all levels how to transition from asanas to meditation. Combining practical advice on breathing and relaxation with timeless asana postures, he systematically guides us through the process. This book provides a five-stage plan to basic meditation, step-by-step guidelines for perfect postures, and six methods for training the breath. Both the novice and the advanced student will benefit from Sovik's startling insights into the mystery of meditation.

Paperback, 6" x 9", 197 pages
$14.95, ISBN 978-0-89389-247-0

To order: 800-822-4547
Email: mailorder@HimalayanInstitute.org
Visit: HimalayanInstitute.org

HIMALAYAN
INSTITUTE®

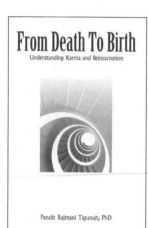

From Death to Birth
Pandit Rajmani Tigunait, PhD

From Death to Birth takes us along the soul's journey from death to birth, dispelling the frequent misconceptions about this subject by revealing little-known but powerful truths. Through a series of lively stories drawn from the ancient scriptures and his own experience, Pandit Tigunait reveals what karma really is, how we can create it, why it becomes our destiny, and how we can use it to shape the future of our dreams.

Paperback, 6" x 9", 216 pages
$15.95, ISBN 978-0-89389-147-3

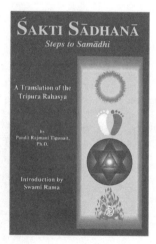

Sakti Sadhana
Pandit Rajmani Tigunait, PhD

The knowledge that enlightens the aspiring student into the mystery of life here and hereafter is the *Tripura Rahasya*. This text is one of the most significant scriptures in the tradition of tantra yoga. Its beauty lies in the fact that it expounds the lofty knowledge of inner truth while systematically offering practical instructions on *sakti sadhana*—the task of awakening the dormant fire within and leading it to higher awareness, or the highest chakra.

Paperback, 6" x 9", 196 pages
$10.95, ISBN 978-0-89389-140-4

To order: 800-822-4547
Email: mailorder@HimalayanInstitute.org
Visit: HimalayanInstitute.org

Yoga and Psychotherapy
The Evolution of Consciousness
Swami Rama, Rudolph Ballentine, MD,
Swami Ajaya, PhD

For thousands of years yoga has offered what Western therapists are currently seeking: a way to achieve the total health of body, mind, emotions, and spirit. *Yoga and Psychotherapy* provides a unique comparison of modern therapy and traditional methods. Drawing upon a rich diversity of experience, the authors give us detailed examples of how the ancient findings of yoga can be used to supplement or replace some of the less complete Western theories and techniques.

Paperback, 6"x 9", 305 pages
$15.95, ISBN 978-0-89389-036-0

Science of Breath
A Practical Guide
Swami Rama, Rudolph Ballentine, MD,
Alan Hymes, MD

Proper breathing helps us achieve physical and mental health and attain higher states of consciousness. *Science of Breath* shows us how. It describes the anatomy and physiology of breathing, as well as the subtle yogic science of prana. Basic yogic breathing techniques are explained so that we can immediately begin working with this powerful science.

Paperback, 6"x 9", 119 pages
$12.95, ISBN 978-0-89389-151-0

To order: 800-822-4547
Email: mailorder@HimalayanInstitute.org
Visit: HimalayanInstitute.org

Radical Healing
Integrating the World's Greatest Therapeutic Traditions To Create a New Transformative Medicine
Rudolph Ballentine, MD

This second edition of *Radical Healing*—revised, expanded, and updated—presents a new vision of health care, one that integrates the holistic traditions of Ayurveda, homeopathy, Traditional Chinese Medicine, and other herbal medicinal traditions. It shows how they overlap, differ, and can be combined for dynamic healing and personal transformation. Includes a Self-Help guide to natural remedies and teatments for over 100 common ailments.

Paperback, 6"x 9", 644 pages
$19.95, ISBN 978-89389-308-8

Transition to Vegetarianism
An Evolutionary Step
Rudolph Ballentine, MD

Written by the author of the popular classics *Diet and Nutrition* and *Radical Healing*, this book explores the health issues surrounding vegetarianism and helps the aspiring vegetarian make the transition in a way that provides the greatest health benefits. *Transition to Vegetarianism* is well researched, easy to ready, and an excellent resource for both the seasoned and would-be vegetarian.

Paperback, 6"x 9", 300 pages
$16.95, ISBN 978-0-89389-104-6

To order: 800-822-4547
Email: mailorder@HimalayanInstitute.org
Visit: HimalayanInstitute.org

HIMALAYAN INSTITUTE®